LAURIE J. SHIFRIN

BATIK BEAUTIES

18 STUNNING QUILTS

Martingale™
& COMPANY

DEDICATION

I dedicate this book to my father, Bernard Shifrin.

ACKNOWLEDGMENTS

Many thanks to

My coworkers and the customers at In The Beginning, who first gave me the encouragement to propose this book to Martingale and then gave me moral support as I worked on the quilts and the text.

Ursula Reikes for being interested in my ideas and for giving me deadlines—without them this book may never have happened.

Trish Carey and Margy Duncan for helping with bindings as well as for their continual interest in the book.

Diane Roubal for making one of the quilts in its entirety.

Gale Whitney for letting me bounce ideas off her.

My good friend Carol Boyer, who helped in many, many ways, including helping me to survive being a first-time computer owner.

Sharon and Jason Yenter for the countless opportunities they have given me to grow as a quilter.

Hoffman California Fabrics for supplying many of the beautiful fabrics you see in this book.

CREDITS

President . . . . Nancy J. Martin
CEO . . . . Daniel J. Martin
Publisher . . . . Jane Hamada
Editorial Director . . . . Mary V. Green
Editorial Project Manager . . . . Tina Cook
Technical Editor . . . . Ursula Reikes
Copy Editor . . . . Candie Frankel
Design and Production Manager . . . . Stan Green
Illustrators . . . . Laurel Strand, Robin Strobel
Cover Designer . . . . Stan Green
Text Designer . . . . Trina Stahl
Photographer . . . . Brent Kane

That Patchwork Place® is an imprint of
Martingale & Company™

Batik Beauties: 18 Stunning Quilts
© 2001 by Laurie Shifrin

Martingale & Company
20205 144th Ave. NE
Woodinville, WA 98072-8478 USA
www.martingale-pub.com

Printed in China
05 04 03 02 01   8 7 6 5 4 3 2 1

MISSION STATEMENT
We are dedicated to providing quality products and service by working together to inspire creativity and to enrich the lives we touch.

Library of Congress Cataloging-in-Publication Data

Shifrin, Laurie.
    Batik beauties / Laurie Shifrin
        p. cm.
        ISBN 1-56477-382-5
        1. Patchwork—Patterns. 2. Quilting—Patterns.
        3. Appliqué—Patterns. 4. Batik. I. Title

TT835 .S4656 2001
746.46'041—dc21   2001030970

CONTENTS

INTRODUCTION

I DIDN'T FALL under the allure of batiks until I started working at In The Beginning, a quilt shop in Seattle, Washington. From my first purchase, I knew it was true infatuation. My collection grew each time a new shipment of batiks arrived, and I started using combinations of batiks in my quiltmaking. These batik quilts got many oohs and ahs from my co-workers and fellow quilters, and before long, the store began using them for displays. This in turn inspired many of our customers to make batik quilts and prompted our staff to find creative ways to package our batiks so that quilters could get little bits of lots of different designs and colors. These fat-quarter packs and fabric rolls sell faster than we can replace them!

I've encountered many quilters who love to collect batiks, but they aren't always sure what to do with them. When I looked for quilt books on the subject, I came up empty-handed. I found books that showed how batiks could add spots of texture or vibrant color but none that featured batiks as the focus of the quilt. Around this time, I attended a class for teachers given by renowned quilter, fabric designer, and author Marsha McCloskey. In class I heard her say we teachers all have at least one quilt book in us. At that time, the idea of writing a book seemed beyond anything I dreamed of in my quilting career. But with encouragement from my friends and coworkers, and interest from Martingale, the rest, as they say, is history.

This book includes step-by-step directions for eighteen quilts. Several of the quilts require appliqué or piecing templates, but most are composed entirely of squares, triangles, and rectangles. You'll be surprised to see how effective even a simple quilt can be using the lush colors and

Enticing packages of batik fabrics are available in many quilt shops.

textures of batiks. Whether you take a scrappy approach and use many different fabrics or limit yourself to four or five fabrics, you'll find batiks make up into a striking quilt. I encourage you to try these patterns with other fabrics from your stash too. Marvelous and unusual effects are possible when you use batiks in combination with traditional fabrics.

I've indicated the required skill level—beginner, intermediate, advanced—for each quilt.

Start with a quilt that matches your skill level and try a more challenging quilt later on. You will find that with accurate seam allowances and pinning where necessary, all of the quilts go together easily with stunning results. To help you get started, I've written advice on choosing and caring for batik fabrics and basic quiltmaking and finishing techniques. Be sure to read these chapters before beginning a project.

I hope that you'll enjoy making the projects in this book and that they will challenge you to stretch your color imagination. My wish is that this book will be a source of inspiration not only to batik lovers, but to fabric lovers everywhere.

Beginner ☐

Intermediate ☐ ◙

Advanced ☐ ◙ ◎

A BRIEF HISTORY OF BATIKS

NO ONE KNOWS exactly where the first batik fabrics were made. The natives of Indonesia have been practicing this type of fabric decorating for centuries, elevating the technique to an art form. Most of the batiks that are produced for quilters are made on the Indonesian island of Bali. Traditional batiks are made on the Indonesian island of Java, where generations-long experience in the art is still a highly valued part of the culture.

The word *batik* is Javanese for "wax writing or painting." Batik is a wax relief method of dyeing and decorating fabric. The melted wax design can be applied in one of two ways. The first and oldest method uses a *tsantung* (pronounced "canting" or "cantung"). This tool looks like a small copper pipe. It holds hot melted wax (a combination of beeswax and paraffin) in a small bowl. The wax flows through one or more small spouts to paint the details of an intricate pattern onto the fabric in a series of lines and dots. Traditionally, the pattern was painted on both sides of the fabric to create a perfect mirror image. This was a painstaking and time-consuming process.

A faster approach, responsible for most of the varied batiks we see in quilting stores today, uses a

ABOVE: *Tsantung*

LEFT: *Traditional batik prints*

stamping tool called a *tsap* (pronounced "cap" or "chop"). A tsap is a block ranging in size from a few inches to about ten inches across. It may be all wood with a design carved on one side, or the wood may have a copper wire design embedded in it. Today, most of the tsaps used to make high-quality batiks are made by soldering the copper wire design to a copper frame; designs can be made more precisely with copper wire than with carved wood. The all-copper tsaps also last longer. The tsap is heated, dipped in hot melted wax, and pressed onto the cloth. Small pins on the block help align the design as the tsap is stamped over and over across the surface of the cloth.

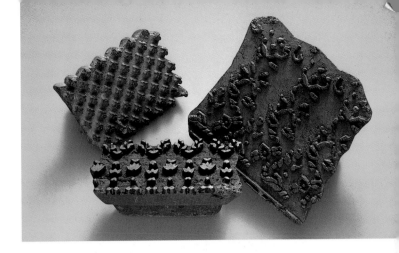

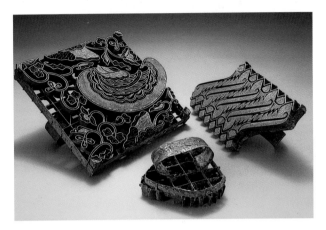

Wood and copper tsaps

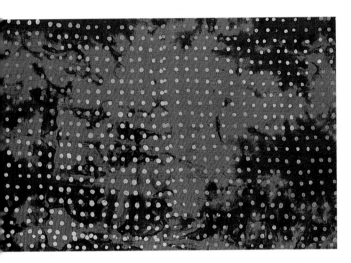

The misaligned dots near the bottom of the photo reveal where the tsap was not aligned correctly.

After the fabric is waxed, it is dipped in or painted with liquid inks and dyes to produce different effects. The waxed areas of the fabric resist absorption of the dye. After drying in the open air, the fabric is submerged in boiling water to melt off the wax, revealing the white, undyed fabric underneath.

The entire process is repeated for each color. For a two-color print, the area that was colored in the first round may be waxed over so that it will not absorb and be affected by the second color. If the colors are meant to blend, then the new wax may be applied, often using a different tsap design, without removing the first wax layer. The number of colors on a batik cloth indicate the number of times it was immersed in dye and how many times the wax was applied and removed.

After the last of the wax is removed, the fabric is dried, pressed, and rolled onto bolts for export around the world. The extensive wetting, boiling, and drying the fabric undergoes make it fairly shrink-resistant when completed.

Today we see an increasing availability of batiks, due in part to the ever growing popularity of quilting and the demand of quilters for new and innovative fabrics. Over the last ten years, the number of fabric companies producing batiks has multiplied from just a few to over a dozen. New techniques, such as rolling or brushing on the wax, have been developed to accommodate changes in technology, but many traditional techniques remain in use.

For more information on batik history and the techniques involved in producing batiks, I recommend the Internet as a primary source. Older books discussing the traditional batik-making processes can be found in public libraries.

A QUILTER'S GUIDE TO BATIKS

RIGHT SIDE OR WRONG SIDE?

IN THE batik-making process, the wax that creates the design sinks into the fabric. As a result, both sides of the fabric show a clear image after dyeing, and it is often hard to tell a difference between the right and wrong side of the fabric. When both sides are virtually identical, I choose the side on which the design is clearer with less-fuzzy edges as the right side. When the colors vary from side to side, I choose the side that better suits my project as the right side. Occasionally, a batik will show a definite right and wrong side. Batik look-alikes often have a definite right and wrong side; be sure to pay attention when cutting these.

WEAVE

THE THREAD count of fabrics commonly used for quilting ranges from the tight weave of pima or lawn to medium-weave poplin to loose-weave sheeting. Some people hesitate to use batiks because they feel the weave is too tight and offers too little give. The fact that batiks are wetted and

In the fabric on the left, the tiny black dots indicate where the wax did not saturate the fabric; this is the wrong side. The clearer design on the right is the right side.

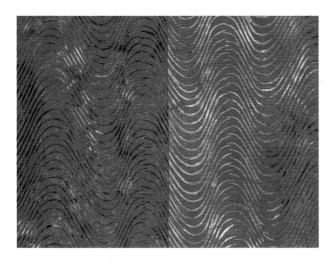

Right side and wrong side. Colors are stronger on the left, but both sides can be used for different looks.

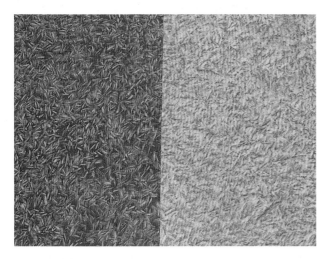

Right side and wrong side of batik look-alike.

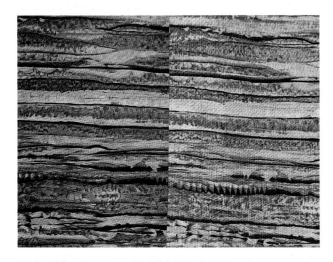

Right side and wrong side of batik look-alike.

dried in the printing process does in fact mean that shrinkage has already occurred—and the weave slightly tightened—before you buy the cloth. As a result, you will experience slightly less give than with other quilting cottons when easing pieces together. But if you cut pieces precisely and sew them with an accurate ¼" seam allowance, they will fit together with no problem.

The tight weave is actually a plus for appliqué work because the edges won't fray when handled. Another benefit is that pieces cut on the bias hardly stretch at all.

Because of the extensive printing process, most batiks have a smooth texture or hand, which in combination with the dense thread count ensures clarity of design.

DYES

THE DYE colors traditionally used for batiks—such as deep indigo blues and rich browns—were made from plants. Plant dyes are still used to color batiks made in Java. However, modern inks and chemical dyes have greatly increased the color range of batiks and improved the color stability. Synthetic dyes bleed less, are more colorfast, and retain their brilliance after washing.

Concerns over colorfastness shouldn't be any more intense with batiks than with any other fabric. Getting the wax off the cloth involves rinsing in boiling hot water, which also washes out most of the excess dye. Still, even the most reputable companies will occasionally produce a batik that bleeds in the wash. Intense blues, reds, and purples are the worst offenders. Prewashing (page 15) is recommended.

BUYING BATIKS

ONE OF the questions commonly asked by quilters is "How much fabric do I buy if I'm not buying for any specific project?" Many of the quilts in this book are scrappy and require little bits of lots of different fabrics. Here are some guidelines to use when purchasing batiks:

- Buy light-colored, solid-looking batiks. They are less common, necessary for contrast, and can often serve as backgrounds. I recommend buying as many of these as your budget permits; 2 to 4 yards of several pieces is a nice amount to have on hand.

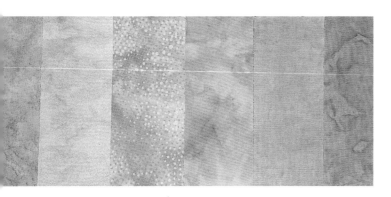

Light background batiks

- Stock up on solid-looking batiks. These batiks are primarily one color and have a texture that is subtle enough to be mistaken as a solid from a distance. If you're adding to your stash, buy ½- to 1-yard pieces.

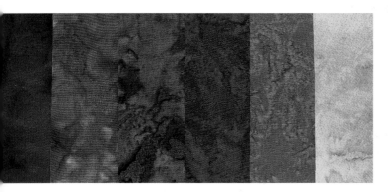

Solid-looking batiks

- Buy any bold print or multicolored large print that appeals to you as a potential border. Buy 3 to 3½ yards to ensure you'll have enough for any size quilt.

- Buy ¼- to ½-yard cuts of batiks that you like, need to have, or envision using in little bits as accents (like bright oranges).

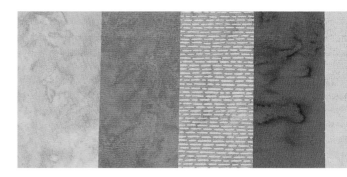

Bright colors for accents

You can place most batiks into one of two categories: mottled or print. Single-color mottled or marbled batiks can be used as solids. Prints can be single-colored or multicolored, and the print can often be described as either textured, geometric, leafy, or ethnic in appearance. Of course, there will be exceptions like the novelty prints shown at bottom of facing page.

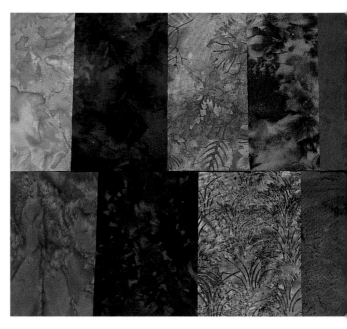

Textured batiks

Geometric batiks

Leaf-print batiks

Ethnic-looking batiks

Novelty batiks

COMBINING BATIKS

WHILE MOST quilters love the look of batiks, they are often not quite sure how to use them. Should they be used only with other batiks, or can they be used in combination with other quilting cottons? Generally, I follow the same rules as I would for any quilting project.

Start by choosing a multicolored print or mottled fabric to use as the main fabric. This print may be larger in scale than the other fabrics that will go into the quilt and it will often end up as the border fabric. Draw on the colors in the main fabric to select coordinating fabrics, being sure to vary the texture, value (lightness to darkness), and scale of print. Include some solid look-alikes and, if possible, some zingers, or contrasting colors, to make your quilt eye-catching. For example, primary colors become zingers when used in combination with black-and-white batiks.

Main fabric and coordinating fabrics

Main fabrics

Nonbatik textures

With nonbatik floral prints, try adding both printed and solid-looking batiks.

Primary colors used as accents with eye-catching black-and-white prints

When mixing batiks with other types of fabrics, explore the many Asian-influenced prints available, such as those used in "Persian Fantasy" (page 103). Contemporary designs and geometric prints look great with almost any batik. To complement a large-print batik, try marbled, mottled, solid, and hand-dyed fabrics.

Batiks coordinated with a nonbatik main fabric

I encourage you to be adventurous and try patterns and colors that stretch your comfort zone. Start with color combinations that please you, but don't feel obligated to stick to your initial selections. It's important that you experiment, try several options, and, most of all, have fun.

Nonbatik main fabrics

THE SCRAPPY LOOK

MANY QUILTERS who are avid fabric collectors love to buy ¼-yard cuts. Several quilts in this book are perfect projects for using up those small quantities of many different fabrics. For quilts with a scrappy look, see "Native Rainbow" (page 37), "Jewels and Jumbles" (page 45), "Modern Mayhem" (page 48), "Mystique of Bali" (page 77), "Glimpse of the Past" (page 81), "Spinning Dreams" (page 89), and "Stepping Out" (page 109).

Detail of "Glimpse of the Past"

Detail of "Native Rainbow"

To decide if a nonscrappy quilt can be made to look scrappy, check to see if there is a repeated block. For example, in "Byzantine Stars" (page 98), you can make all the blocks as shown, make them all different, or make a few from each of a few fabrics and mix them up. The key to creating an effective scrappy look is to distribute like fabrics and colors evenly throughout the quilt while avoiding perfect symmetry. Think of tossing a handful of multicolored toothpicks in the air and letting them fall in a random pattern. That is the look you should try to achieve when placing your fabrics.

Another opportunity to add a scrappy look to a quilt is in a pieced border. Many different fabrics are used for the small squares in the second border of "Native Rainbow." The outer border of "Stepping Out" is also made from several different fabrics.

Of course, you can also reverse the approach and rework a scrappy design in just a few fabrics. Try making "Mystique of Bali" with all of the flying geese from one fabric or "Modern Mayhem" using one print for all the larger squares, a second print for the rectangles, and a third print for the small squares. All the star blocks in "Jewels and Jumbles" could be made with just three fabrics, and the sashing triangles from a limited number of fabrics.

Detail of "Byzantine Stars"

FABRIC PREPARATION

ALL FABRICS, including batiks, should be pre-washed in order to preshrink them, remove any sizing that may have been added during the man-ufacturing process, and test for colorfastness. You can prewash fabrics by hand or machine. Keep similar values and colors together and wash the fabrics on a short gentle cycle, using a small amount of commercial detergent or, preferably, a gentle soap made especially for quilting fabrics. Use cool water and check the water during the final rinse to see if it is running clear (no color). If it isn't, put the fabric through another rinse cycle. Continue until the water runs clear. If you come across a fabric that continues to bleed, add a cup of white vinegar to the rinse water to help set the dye. There are also chemical products available at your quilt shop that aid in removing excess dye and setting the color in the fabric.

To dry fabrics, I recommend using the hot set-ting on the dryer. Run the cycle until the fabric is almost dry, to encourage the most shrinkage. To prevent wrinkles from setting, remove the fabric promptly before it has a chance to sit in the dryer. Using a hot iron, press the entire length of fabric, always parallel to the selvage.

For each quilt in this book, the yardage amounts listed under "Materials" allow for shrink-age and straightening and assume a 40" fabric width after prewashing. If your fabric measures less than 40" wide after preshrinking, you may need additional fabric. Note that directional designs may also require additional fabric and/or a change in the cutting directions.

BASIC QUILTMAKING TECHNIQUES

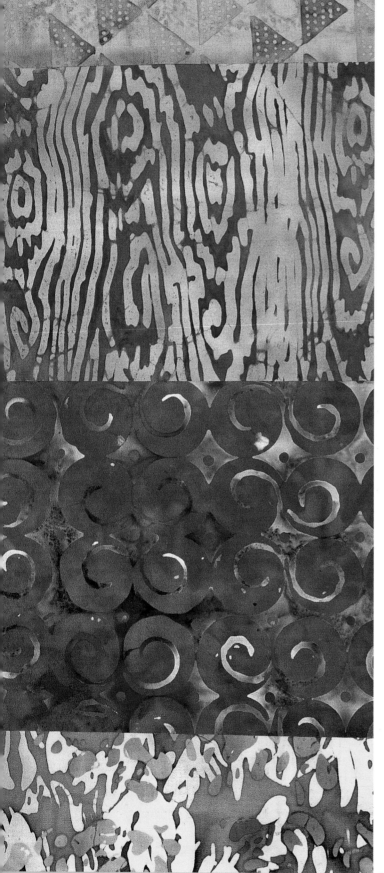

TOOLS

- Sewing machine in good working order.
- Rotary cutter, medium size (45mm).
- Self-healing cutting mat, 18" x 24".
- Acrylic ruler, 6" x 24" with a 45° line.
- Sharp sewing shears for cutting fabric.
- Small scissors with a pointed tip for appliqué and clipping threads.
- Utility scissors for cutting template plastic.
- Seam ripper to remove stitches before resewing a seam.

- Thin 1⅜"-long pins with round glass heads; the thin shaft slides easily through the fabric and seams.
- Short appliqué pins for appliquéing.
- Template plastic material for machine-piecing templates.
- Sharp pencil.
- Design wall for arranging and viewing blocks (or an entire quilt) before sewing; particularly useful when working with scrappy fabrics.
- Appliqué needles, also called Sharps.
- Sewing-machine needles, size 12 universal or Sharps, for piecing and quilting. Change your machine needle after eight hours of sewing or before every new project.
- Long needles for basting layers together. I recommend milliner's needles.
- Thimble for handwork. A thimble should fit securely on the middle finger of your dominant hand. Thimbles with indented tops are much easier to use because the rim gives the needle a place to rest.
- Iron and ironing board, set up near your sewing machine.
- Mini Iron by Clover. This little iron is especially useful for appliqué projects.
- Thread for machine or hand piecing. May be 100 percent cotton or cotton-covered polyester, but be aware that the polyester thread, being stronger, may wear through the fibers of the cotton cloth over time.
- Thread for hand appliqué. The thread should match the color of the appliqué pieces, not the background. A finer weight thread (size 60) will help make the stitches invisible. I love the fine silk thread from YLI for hand appliqué. It seems to sink into the fabric and disappear.
- ¹⁄₁₆" hole punch for marking intersecting points on plastic templates; available at office supply or stationery stores.

ROTARY CUTTING

THE BASIC rotary-cutting tools include a rotary cutter, an 18" x 24" rotary-cutting mat, and a 6" x 24" acrylic ruler. This size ruler will get you through all of the projects in this book.

Correct use of your rotary cutter starts with respecting the blade. Keep the safety catch closed. Expose the blade only when you are actually making the cut, and then close the blade immediately after. Keep the cutter away from children and pets, and dispose of old blades safely.

Before you can rotary-cut fabric, you need to get it properly aligned. When you prewash fabric, the selvages shrink differently from the rest of the goods and tend to pucker and pull. To compensate for the distortion, fold the fabric in half lengthwise by bringing the two selvages together; then make a second fold by bringing the folded edge almost to the selvages. Now you can use the two folded edges for alignment and ignore the crooked selvages.

Place the folded fabric on the cutting mat with the raw edge to the right. Place the ruler on the fabric, near the right raw edge, and align one of the horizontal grid lines of the ruler on the fold nearest you. Hold the ruler in place with your left hand, keeping your pinkie on the fabric next to the left edge of the ruler. Trim the uneven raw edge of the fabric using the rotary cutter. Use even pressure on the blade and roll the cutter *away from you*, keeping it pressed against the ruler as you go.

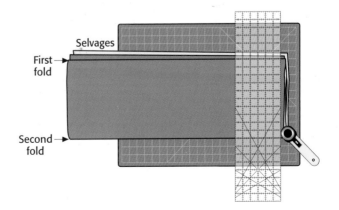

Selvages

First fold

Second fold

Rotate the mat and fabric 180° so the clean-cut edge is on the left. (It may be necessary to fold the fabric on top of itself and pile it on the mat.) To cut a strip, line up the required measurement on the ruler with the clean-cut edge of the fabric. For example, if you want a 3"-wide strip, place the 3" ruler mark on the edge of the fabric. Remember to align a horizontal grid line on the ruler with the folded edge. Cut the strip.

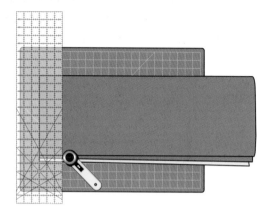

To cut a strip into pieces, place the strip horizontally on the mat, with one selvage to the right. Trim off the selvage or rough edge as you did when you trimmed the uneven edge. Turn the mat around so the clean-cut edge is on the left. Place the ruler so that a horizontal line is even with the long edge of the fabric and the desired vertical line is even with the left edge, and cut.

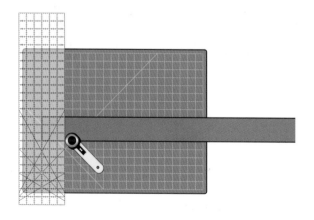

MACHINE PIECING

THE MOST important aspect of machine piecing is to sew with an accurate ¼" seam allowance. If your seam allowance is off slightly, even by a few threads, your blocks may not fit together well and this will in turn affect other steps in the quilt top assembly. Some machines have a special presser foot that measures exactly ¼" from the center needle position to the edge of the foot. This allows you to use the edge of the foot as a guide for the fabric to get a perfect ¼" seam allowance. On some machines, you can move the needle position left or right so that the distance between the needle and the edge of the presser foot is ¼".

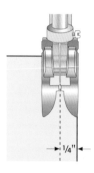

TIP: I use a scant ¼" seam allowance (1 or 2 threads of the fabric less than ¼") to accommodate what's lost in pressing.

If your machine doesn't have either of these features, you can create a seam guide by placing a piece of tape or moleskin or a magnetic seam guide ¼" from the needle.

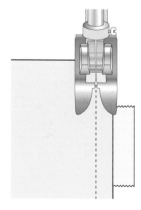

Use a small stitch length (10 to 12 stitches per inch). It is not necessary to backstitch at the beginning or end of seams. However, I recommend reducing the stitch length for the last ½" on seams that extend to the outside edge of the quilt top. This adds a little extra stability to the seams at the outside edges.

TIP: Use a seam ripper to remove unwanted stitching. To avoid stretching the fabric, cut the thread every 4 or 5 stitches on one side of the fabric. Then, on the reverse side, pull up on the thread. It should come out easily.

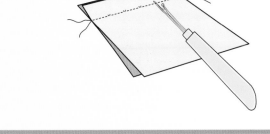

Chain Piecing

Chain piecing is a machine-piecing method that lets you sew fabric pieces together quickly. To chain-piece, sew the first pair of pieces from cut edge to cut edge. Stop sewing at the end of the seam, but do not cut the thread. Feed the next pair of pieces under the presser foot, close to the preceding pair. Continue feeding pieces through the machine without cutting the thread. When all pieces are sewn, remove the chain from the machine and clip the threads between the pairs of sewn pieces.

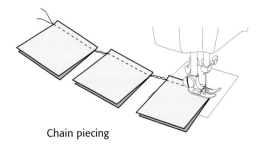

Chain piecing

Easing

Occasionally, it becomes necessary to ease fabric when sewing two pieces together. This occurs when the edge of one piece is slightly longer than the other because of cutting discrepancies, seam width variations, or different fabric grains. To ease, pin the pieces together at the seams and ends and in between, if necessary, to distribute the excess fabric. With the shorter piece on top, stitch the seam. The feed dogs will ease the fullness of the longer piece, while the presser foot will lengthen the top piece.

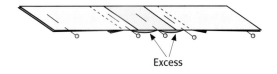

Excess

PRESSING

Use a hot iron on the cotton setting. Pressing arrows are included in the diagrams when it is necessary to press the seams in a particular direction. When no arrows are indicated, the direction of the seam allowance does not matter.

In general, seams should be pressed in opposite directions wherever two seams meet. This technique, called butting, helps the fabric to lie flat and gives a more accurate match, yielding perfect intersections. Press seams toward the darker fabric or toward the section with fewer seams, unless otherwise indicated. Press after each step.

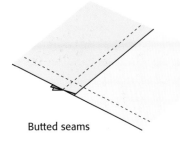

Butted seams

HALF-SQUARE AND QUARTER-SQUARE TRIANGLES

SEVERAL OF the quilts in this book are made with half-square and quarter-square triangles. The difference between the two is the position of the straight grain and bias grain. On half-square triangles, the straight grain is on the short sides of the triangle and the bias is on the long side. On quarter-square triangles, the straight grain is on the long side of the triangle and the bias is on the short sides. Follow the directions below for making half-square- and quarter-square-triangle units.

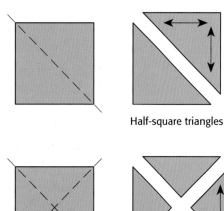

Half-square triangles

Quarter-square triangles

Detail of "Jewels and Jumbles"

Half-Square-Triangle Units

1. Cut squares the size specified in the cutting list. (This measurement equals the finished short side of the triangle + ⅞".)

2. Pair squares right sides together, placing the lighter fabric on top. With a sharp pencil, mark a diagonal line from corner to corner on the wrong side of the lighter fabric. Sew ¼" on each side of the diagonal line.

3. Cut on the marked line through both layers. Press seams toward the darker fabric. Trim the dog-ears. Each pair of squares will yield 2 half-square-triangle units.

Quarter-Square-Triangle Units

1. Cut squares the size specified in the directions. (This measurement equals the finished long edge of the triangle + 1¼".)

2. Pair squares right sides together, placing the lighter fabric on top. With a sharp pencil, mark a diagonal line from corner to corner on the wrong side of the lighter fabric. Sew ¼" on each side of the diagonal line.

3. Rotary cut on the *unmarked* diagonal. Then cut on the marked diagonal line. Press the seams toward the darker fabric. Trim the dog-ears.

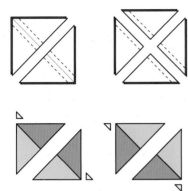

4. Use units as cut in step 3, or pair 2 units together to form a quarter-square-triangle unit. For a scrappy look, mix up the pairs of fabric squares and then mix up the triangle pairs.

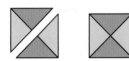

Multiple Half-Square-Triangle Units

Use the following quick method when a pattern calls for multiple (more than ten) half-square-triangle units made from two fabrics. Cut the required number of strips of each fabric, but do not crosscut them into squares. Instead:

1. Place the strips right sides together, lighter fabric on top. With a sharp pencil, mark perpendicular lines to divide the lighter strip into segments the same size as the strip width. For example, if the strip is 2½" wide, mark lines at 2½" intervals.

2. Mark a diagonal line in each segment, forming a zigzag pattern across the squares. Sew ¼" on each side of the diagonal lines.

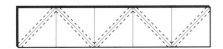

3. Rotary cut along the perpendicular segment lines, and then along the diagonal lines. Press, and trim the dog-ears.

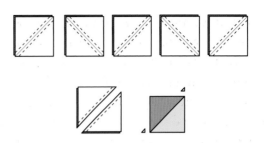

Multiple Quarter-Square-Triangle Units

The method for making multiple quarter-square-triangle units is similar to the half-square method described previously. Cut the required number of strips of each fabric. Follow steps 1 and 2 for "Multiple Half-Square-Triangle Units." For step 3, rotary cut along the perpendicular lines, but before cutting on the marked diagonal lines, cut each square in half on the opposite diagonal—the one without the marked line. Then cut on the marked diagonal to yield the quarter-square-triangle units. Press, and trim the dog-ears.

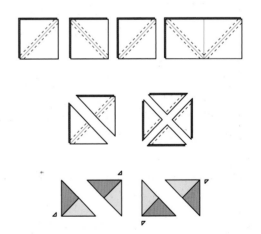

MACHINE-PIECING TEMPLATES

"Byzantine Stars" (page 98) has odd-shaped pieces that must be cut using piecing templates. Trace each pattern piece onto template plastic. Use utility scissors to cut out the pieces on the outside line. On the right side of the template, mark the quilt name, the piece number or letter, and the grain line. Mark the seam intersections using a 1/16" hole punch. When using templates to cut fabric, pay careful attention to the grain line noted on the template. With a pencil, trace the shape of the template onto the fabric and cut out on the drawn line.

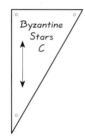

Some patterns call for fabric pieces to be cut from the templates as pictured *and* reversed. When a template piece must be cut in reverse, simply turn the template over and place it right side down on the fabric. An "r" following the template letter is used to indicate a reversed piece.

APPLIQUÉ

I recommend the freezer-paper method for the appliqué project in this book, "Spring Rendezvous" (page 93).

1. Place the freezer paper shiny side down on the pattern, and trace on the dull, paper side using a pencil. Cut out the design on the pencil line; do not add seam allowance. If you need multiple copies of the same pattern piece, staple up to 4 layers of freezer paper together and cut them simultaneously. To cut reversed templates when called for, place the freezer paper dull side down and trace on the shiny side. After cutting

and removing the staples, mark the right (dull) side of each template with the piece name.

2. Place the shiny side of the freezer-paper template on the right side of the fabric. Press with a hot, dry iron for 1 to 2 seconds. Cut out the fabric shape, adding a 1/4" seam allowance all around the outside edge of the freezer paper.

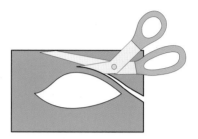

Cut 1/4" from edge of freezer paper.

3. Peel off the freezer-paper template and place the paper's dull side against the wrong side of the fabric, centering the template on the fabric shape. Using the tip of your iron or mini iron, press the fabric seam allowance over the edge of the freezer paper. Be careful not to shift the paper as you go.

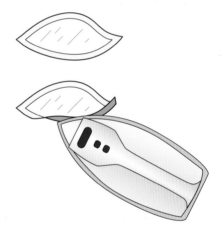

Fold the outside points as shown.

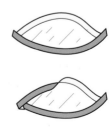

4. Pin the pieces in place to the background fabric and then baste with thread and needle. If you want to skip the basting step, use short appliqué pins so your thread won't get caught.

5. Appliqué each piece in the recommended order, using a small blind hem stitch, tucking in the corner seam allowance as you go.

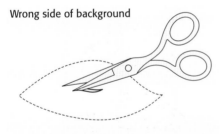

6. Remove pins or basting stitches. Working from the back, use small, sharp scissors to cut a ½" slit in the background fabric behind the appliqué. Be careful not to cut into the appliquéd piece. Carefully remove the freezer paper using tweezers (you may have to tug a little if you have stitched through the paper). Press when completed.

Wrong side of background

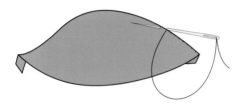

ASSEMBLING THE BLOCKS

WHEN YOU have made all the blocks and cut all the remaining pieces, it's time to put everything together.

Straight-Set Quilts

Arrange the blocks, referring to the quilt photograph and diagram provided with each quilt. Sew the blocks together in horizontal rows. Press the seams in opposite directions from row to row, unless otherwise indicated. Sew the rows together, matching and pinning seams. Press the row seams in one direction.

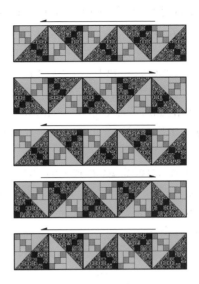

Diagonally Set Quilts

Arrange the blocks and side and corner triangles, referring to the quilt photograph and diagram provided with each quilt. Sew the blocks and side triangles together in diagonal rows. Press the seams as indicated in the assembly diagram for your quilt. Sew the rows together, matching and pinning seams. Press the row seams in one direction. Add the corner triangles last.

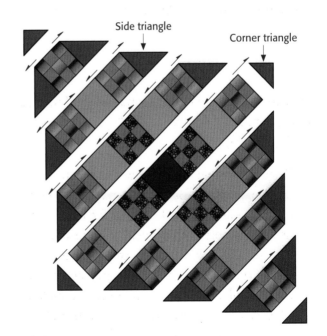

Side triangle

Corner triangle

Changing the Size of a Quilt

If the size or shape of a quilt in this book isn't exactly what you need, look first at the possibility of adding or subtracting blocks or rows from the center of the quilt. That may require some math on your part; I suggest you overestimate your fabric needs when adding or subtracting to change the size of a quilt.

If the design doesn't lend itself to that approach, then try making the border wider or narrower. For those quilts that are easily adjustable, I have offered tips for changing the size.

BORDERS

You will notice that each quilt in this book features its own unique border. Just as quilting styles have evolved, so should our approach to borders. My goal has been to make the border a continuation or extension of the design in the center of the quilt top. I offer border options that go beyond the traditional, and I encourage you to use these variations in future projects.

For best results, even if the measurements for the border strips are given in the quilt instructions, you should measure your quilt top before cutting the borders. Follow the basic directions below for attaching straight-cut borders and mitered borders.

Straight-Cut Borders

Cut strips on either the crosswise or lengthwise grain as specified in the quilt directions. For large quilts, border strips cut on the crosswise grain will need to be pieced together end to end to make one long strip. Measure the length of the quilt top through the center from top to bottom. (The edges of the quilt tend to be longer than the measurement through the center of the quilt.) Cut two border strips to that length; this includes the seam allowance.

Fold each strip in half to find the middle; mark with a sharp pencil or a pin. Also mark the middle of each side edge of the quilt top. Pin the borders to the sides of the quilt top, matching the midpoints and ends. Pin along the entire edge, easing as necessary. With the border strip on top, sew each border in place. Press the seams toward the border unless otherwise noted.

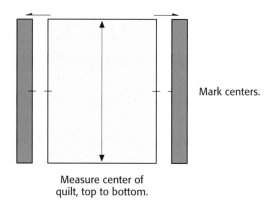

Mark centers.

Measure center of
quilt, top to bottom.

Measure the width of the quilt top through the center, including the side borders you just added. Cut two border strips to that measurement and follow the steps in the previous paragraph to mark, pin, and sew the borders to the top and bottom edges.

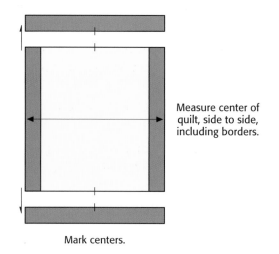

Measure center of
quilt, side to side,
including borders.

Mark centers.

Mitered Borders

Mitered corners add finesse to a finished quilt and are worth the extra effort. Miters are especially effective when you are using stripes. When a quilt has multiple borders, sew the individual strips together and treat the resulting unit as a single piece for mitering. Butting the seams of multiple borders will give a better match at the corners. To do this, press the seams of the side border strips in one direction—for example, toward the center of the quilt top—and the seams of the top and bottom border strips in the opposite direction (away from the center). This is not always possible to achieve. Extremely thin border strips can be difficult to press in the desired direction. You can press them all in the same direction and flip back the seam allowances at the corners to make the miter, or you can make the miter with the seams all going in the same direction. Careful pinning will ensure a clean corner.

Follow these simple directions to produce perfect miters every time.

1. Measure the width of the quilt top through the center. To this measurement, add 2 times the width of the border + 4" extra. For example, if your quilt top is 20" wide and you are adding a 3" border, you would cut 2 strips 30" long for the top and bottom borders.

$$20" + 3" + 3" + 4" = 30"$$

2. Measure the length of the quilt top and repeat the process to cut the side borders.

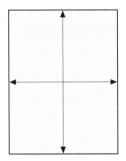

3. On the wrong side of the quilt top, mark the middle of each edge with a sharp pencil or pin. Also mark ¼" in from each edge at the corners.

4. Divide the quilt top width in half and subtract ¼" for the seam allowance.

$$20" \div 2 = 10"$$
$$10" - ¼" = 9¾"$$

Fold the top border strip in half to find the middle; mark with a sharp pencil or a pin. Measure out in both directions from the midpoint and mark the length you just calculated. Repeat to mark the remaining 3 border strips.

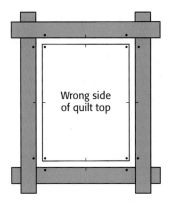

5. Pin 1 border strip to its corresponding side of the quilt top, matching the middle and end marks. Pin every 3" to 4", easing in fullness if necessary. With the border strip on top, sew from one ¼" corner mark to the other, backstitching at each end. Repeat for the remaining border strips, being careful not to catch in previously sewn pieces. Press the seams toward the borders.

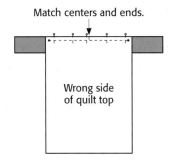

Match centers and ends.

Wrong side of quilt top

6. To make the miter, fold the quilt top diagonally, right sides together, with the border edge toward you. Line up the border strip seams and edges. Push the border seam allowances toward the center of the quilt top. Insert a pin along the border seam. Place a second pin in the excess border fabric and a third pin along the folded edge.

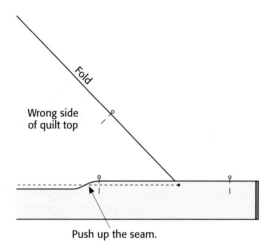

7. Place the ruler on the fabric so the long edge is on the fold and the 45° line is on the border edge. Mark a line on the border strip with a pencil, starting where the stitching leaves off. Pin along this line.

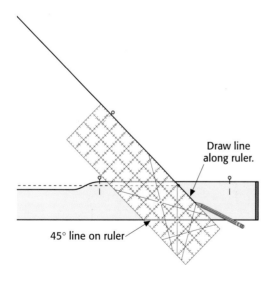

8. Starting with a backstitch, sew on the marked line from the seam endpoint to the border edge.

> TIP: Rather than end this seam with a backstitch, which often distorts the corner, I recommend reducing the stitch length over the last half inch of the seam.

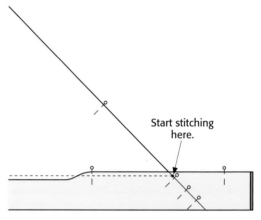

9. Remove all pins, open the seam, and check to see if the mitered corner lies flat. Trim the seam allowance to ¼". Press the mitered seam to one side; press the seam allowance of the borders back down. Repeat to miter the remaining corners.

FINISHING

TOOLS

- Masking tape to secure the backing when layering the quilt sandwich, and for marking straight quilting lines.
- Size 2 safety pins for basting the layers together for machine quilting.
- Plastic quilting templates; use either purchased ready-made templates, available in many sizes and designs, or make your own by tracing your design onto mesh transfer canvas by Clover or examining-room paper.
- Blue washout markers, silver pencils, chalk pencils (nonwaxy type), and chalk tools (like the Chaco-Liner) for transferring quilting designs to the quilt top.
- Quilting needles, size 9 or 10, for hand quilting; also called Betweens.
- Thimble for hand quilting. A thimble should fit securely on the middle finger of your dominant hand. Thimbles with indented tops are much easier to use because the rim gives the needle a place to rest.
- Thread for hand quilting. Many people use only 100 percent–cotton quilting thread for hand quilting. This necessitates the use of thread wax or a comparable synthetic product

like Thread Heaven to strengthen the thread so it slides through the fabric easily. I prefer cotton-covered polyester thread because it doesn't need waxing and it rarely knots or frays. Be aware that the polyester thread, because it is stronger, may wear through the fibers of the cotton cloth over time.

- Walking foot for machine quilting straight lines and gentle curves.
- Darning foot for free-motion quilting.
- Hoop or quilting frame if desired.

THE QUILT SANDWICH

ONCE THE quilt top is complete, it is time to layer the top, batting, and backing. Cut your backing at least 4" larger than the top on all sides. Larger quilts may require a pieced back. It is acceptable to place the seams vertically or horizontally; whichever requires fewer seams and makes more economical use of the fabric. Trim all selvages before sewing the seams for the backing. Press the seams open if you are hand quilting, to distribute bulk. Press to one side if you are machine quilting.

Scrappy backings are another option. They can be fun when made from leftover fabrics from the quilt top. If you need only a few more inches of fabric, just add a strip of another fabric. Be aware that the additional layers of fabric at every seam can make hand quilting difficult.

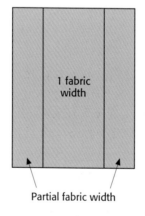

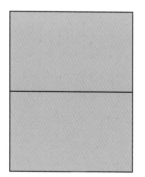

Horizontally pieced back

1 fabric width

Partial fabric width

Tape the backing, right side down, to a table or work surface large enough to fit the entire back. Begin by taping the middle of one side and then the middle of the opposite side, being careful not to stretch the fabric. Then tape the centers of the two remaining sides. Continue taping each edge from the middle out, about 6" apart, always working opposite sides.

Carefully unfold the batting. Be careful not to pull too hard, to avoid creating thin spots. Place the batting over the back. If you need to shift the batting, pretend you are placing a sheet on a bed; get air under it to move it. Don't drag the batting across the backing fabric; you may dislodge it. Once the batting is in place, smooth out any wrinkles by gently brushing your hands over the surface, from the center out. Be careful not to stretch the batting. Trim any excess that is larger than the backing.

Place the well-pressed quilt top right side up over the batting, keeping the edges of the top parallel to the edges of the backing. Smooth from the center out, and along straight lines (like the inner borders) to ensure they remain straight.

If you are hand quilting, baste the layers together using quilting thread and a long needle. Take long running stitches and work from the center out, basting to each corner. Then baste a grid of horizontal and vertical lines 4" to 6" apart. Finally, baste around the perimeter of the quilt top, within ¼" of the edge.

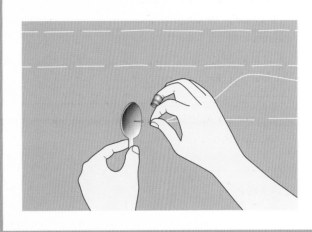

TIP: Try using a teaspoon to lift the needle for an easier grip.

If you intend to machine quilt, use #2 rust-proof safety pins to baste the layers together, placing the pins 4" to 6" apart. Try to avoid areas you intend to quilt.

BATTING

WHEN CHOOSING the batting for your quilt, consider the following:

- Will you be hand or machine quilting the project?
- Will you hang the quilt on a wall, or do you expect to use it?
- How "drapey" or how "poofy" would you like the quilt to be?

Generally, the thinner the batting, the easier it is to hand quilt. You can choose either cotton or polyester; both are a pleasure to use. Avoid cotton battings that have a scrim, or a thin mesh that the fibers are woven through. A scrim helps stabilize the batting, but it can be difficult to hand quilt. Heavily bonded polyester battings present a similar problem. The same bonded finish that prevents batting fibers from coming through the surface of the quilt can hamper hand quilting. Thin

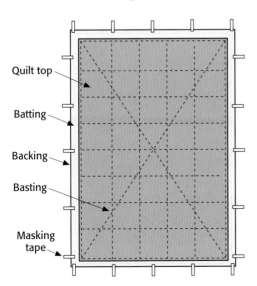

Quilt top

Batting

Backing

Basting

Masking tape

to medium thicknesses of both types of batting can be used for machine quilting. Thick polyester battings with lots of loft or "poof" are used mostly for tied quilts. Cotton and polyester blends (80 percent cotton and 20 percent polyester) are also popular with many quilters. They are easy to quilt, they give the look and feel of a 100 percent–cotton batting, and the quilting stands out a bit more because the polyester has a little loft to it.

If you want the quilt to "melt" or drape over the bed, use cotton batting. For wall hangings, use cotton or polyester battings that are not too thin, or else the quilt will not lie flat on the wall.

I recommend that you try as many battings as possible so that you can be familiar enough with them to choose the right one for each project.

MARKING THE QUILT TOP

MARKING THE top is not always necessary. If you are stitching in the ditch, outlining appliqué pieces, or meandering in a random fashion, marking is not needed. More detailed quilt designs do need to be marked. Depending on which marking tool you use, you may want to mark before the top is layered with the batting and back, or after the quilt sandwich is prepared.

Use a marking tool that will be clearly visible on your fabrics. Always test the tool on a scrap of each fabric, to be sure the marks can be removed easily later on. For marking medium to dark fabrics, I like a chalk tool that dispenses powdered chalk in a thin line. As these products are designed to wipe away after you're done quilting, you must mark your lines after the quilt sandwich is layered. For marking light fabrics, I prefer a blue washout marker. It makes a visible line and can be marked before or after the quilt sandwich is layered. There have been warnings that these products leave chemical residue on the fabric that may turn brown in the future. To prevent this from happening, rinse the entire quilt in clear water (no soap) when you are completely done quilting. This will get the chemical out of the fabric and batting.

You can also use a silver pencil to mark quilting lines. Keep the tip very sharp, and use a light touch; you can mark both light and dark fabrics. Silver marks are permanent but are the least visible of the pencil options. You can use masking tape to mark straight quilting lines, but be sure to remove the tape at the end of each day to prevent a sticky residue on the fabric.

QUILTING

WHEN DECIDING on your quilting designs, consider the desired effect. In most cases, batiks are so gorgeous, they speak for themselves and need little quilted enhancement. Other than securing the quilt sandwich, not much is required. The most common kind of quilting, stitch in the ditch, neither adds nor detracts from the pieced design. It is done by stitching along the seams, on the side away from the seam allowance.

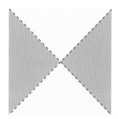

To decide how much quilting is needed, use the general rule that any unquilted spaces should be no bigger than your fist, or about 4" x 4". Quilting closely will prevent sagging in unquilted areas and prevent excess stress on the fabric and quilting thread. Additionally, if the quilt is ever washed, you can be confident the batting will hold together.

Another basic guideline is that the quantity of quilting should be similar throughout the entire top. This ensures that the quilt will remain square and not get distorted after being quilted. A very common mistake is to quilt heavily toward the center of the quilt top in the patchwork area and do very little quilting in the border. This will definitely lead to a wavy border!

A nice way to add to the overall design of your quilt is to turn design elements from the batik prints into quilting motifs. Here are some examples:

Detail of "Trip to Indonesia"

Detail of "Fire Dance"

Detail of "Byzantine Stars"

Detail of "Mystique of Bali"

should always enhance the quilt rather than distract the viewer.

Quilting designs such as the flames in "Fire Dance" or the pools of water in "Mystique of Bali" can be used to emphasize the theme or feel of the quilt. But in most of these batik quilts, there is enough going on that little quilting is needed to make the quilt exciting. As a rule, the quilting

Hand Quilting

To quilt by hand, use a quilting needle, quilting thread, and a thimble as described in "Tools" (page 27). Many quilters use a hoop or frame to support their work, but you can quilt without one provided your quilt has been well-basted. The following steps explain how to hand quilt. For more information on hand quilting, refer to *Loving Stitches: A Guide to Fine Hand Quilting* by Jeanna Kimball (That Patchwork Place, 1992).

1. Thread your needle with a single strand of quilting thread about 18" long. Make a small knot and insert the needle in the top layer about 1" from the place where you want to start stitching. Pull the needle out at the point where the quilting will begin and gently pull the thread until the knot pops through the fabric and into the batting.

2. Take small, evenly spaced stitches through all 3 layers of the quilt. Rock the needle up and down through all layers until you have 3 or 4 stitches on the needle. Place your other hand underneath the quilt so you can feel the point of the needle with the tip of your first finger when a stitch is taken.

3. To end a line of quilting, make a small knot close to the last stitch; then backstitch, running the thread a needle's length through the batting. Gently pull the thread until the knot pops into the batting; clip the thread at the quilt's surface.

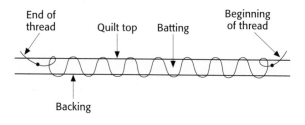

End of thread / Quilt top / Batting / Beginning of thread

Backing

TIP: If you aren't using a frame and can easily turn the area you are quilting upside down, then you can make both the starting and ending knots from the backside of the quilt.

Machine Quilting

Machine quilting lets you complete your projects quickly and is suitable for all types of quilts. For quilting straight lines, a walking foot is a must; it will let you feed quilt layers evenly through the machine without puckering. If your machine doesn't have a built-in walking foot, you will need a separate attachment.

For free-motion quilting, you will need a darning foot and the ability to drop the feed dogs on your machine. Guide the fabric under the needle in the direction of the design. This approach is very useful if you want to stitch over a design in a fabric or to create curved patterns.

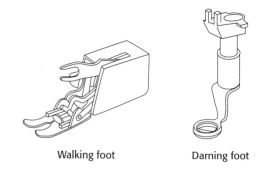

Walking foot   Darning foot

For more information on machine quilting, refer to *Machine Quilting Made Easy* by Maurine Noble (That Patchwork Place, 1994).

BINDING

AFTER YOU have finished quilting your project, the final step is to bind the raw edges. I prefer double-fold binding for a fuller-looking, better-wearing edge. You can cut binding strips on the straight grain or on the bias. Bias will wear better and last longer on quilts that are handled frequently. Straight-grain binding will help make the edges of a wall hanging more square. The yardages given for binding are for cutting straight-grain strips. To cut bias strips for bias binding, buy an additional ⅛ yard of binding fabric.

For straight-grain, double-fold binding, cut 2½"-wide strips from selvage to selvage. You need enough strips to go around the perimeter of the quilt top plus about 20" to allow for seams and finishing.

To cut strips for bias binding, place the 45° line of the ruler along the edge of the fabric and trim off about 10" at one corner. Cut 2½"-wide strips parallel to the diagonal cut edge. When the edge becomes too long for the ruler, fold the fabric and align the cut edges as shown. Continue cutting until you have enough strips to go around the quilt top plus about 20".

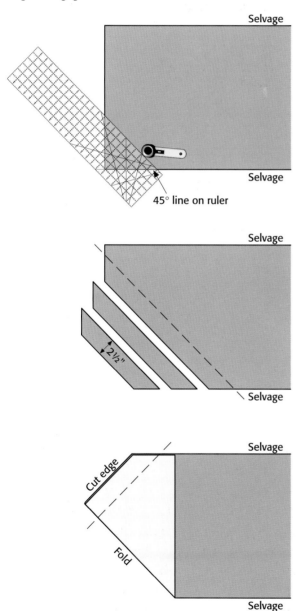

NOTE: *To add a hanging sleeve with the binding, see page 35.*

Attach the binding (straight grain or bias) as follows:

1. Join strips end to end with a diagonal seam. Trim the seam allowance to ¼". Press the seams open.

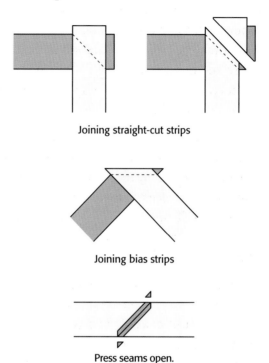

Joining straight-cut strips

Joining bias strips

Press seams open.

2. Press the binding in half lengthwise, wrong side in.

3. Set the machine to a slightly longer stitch length (8 to 10 stitches per inch) and attach the walking foot. Starting near the middle of one side, align the raw edges of the binding with the edge of the quilt top. Leave a 6" tail of binding free. Stitch toward the corner with a ¼" seam. As you come near the corner, insert a pin ¼" from the lower edge. Sew up to that pin and take a few backstitches.

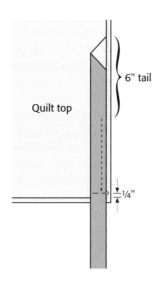

4. Without clipping the thread, take the needle out of the fabric, lift the presser foot and turn the quilt 90° counterclockwise, as if you were continuing on the next side. Fold the binding up and then down, even with the top edge. Start sewing again at the top edge. Repeat this process at each corner.

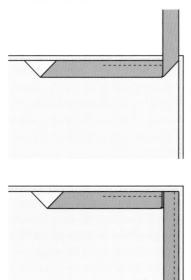

5. Stop sewing about 7" from where you began. Trim the start tail to about 1½" from where you stopped. Lay it flat on the quilt top. Overlap the end tail over the start tail. Trim the end tail so that the overlap measures 2½".

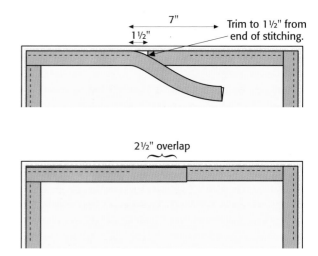

6. In your left hand, open the end tail so the right side is toward you. In your right hand, open the start tail so the wrong side is toward you. Overlap the ends at a right angle, right sides together. Secure with 3 pins. Mark the diagonal for a stitching line.

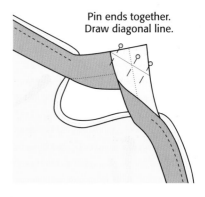

7. Stitch on the marked line. Check to make sure you've stitched correctly, and then trim the seam allowance to ¼". Finger-press the seam open. Refold the binding in half. Lay the binding flat along the edge and finish sewing the binding to the quilt top.

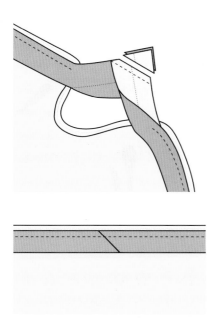

8. Trim the batting and backing slightly larger (about ⅛") than the quilt top—a good binding is one that is full of batting. You may need to trim the batting and backing a little more or a little less depending on the thickness of the batting you use.

9. Bring the binding around to the back and pin, making sure the binding covers the machine stitching. Using a blind hem stitch, secure the binding to the back by hand. Miter the corners.

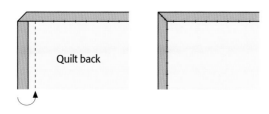

HANGING SLEEVES

ONE OF the simplest ways to hang your quilt is by attaching a fabric sleeve to the back, putting a dowel though the sleeve, and resting the dowel on two nails in the wall.

Cut a piece of fabric 6" wide by the width of the quilt, piecing if necessary. Fold and press the short ends 1" to the wrong side. Fold the piece in half lengthwise, right side out. Pin the two raw edges of the sleeve to the back of the quilt within ¼" from the edge of the top. Sew this edge in place when you attach the binding.

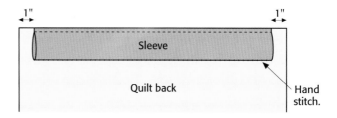

Sew the folded edge to the quilt with a blind hem stitch, being careful not to go through the front of the quilt. Have your local hardware store or lumberyard cut a ½"- to ¾"-diameter dowel the width of the top minus 1". Slip the dowel through the sleeve; hang over two flat-head nails.

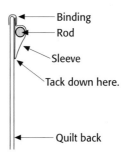

LABELS

PART OF the pleasure of completing a quilt is adding a label to the back of the quilt. A label provides documentation of important information, including the name of the quilt, who made it, for whom, when, and where. All who see or own the quilt in years to come will treasure this information.

A label can be as simple or as elaborate as you want to make it. Use a permanent marking tool such as a Pigma Micron pen. To keep the fabric from shifting as you write, tape it to your work surface or iron it to a piece of freezer paper. To help me keep my writing straight, I draw lines on a piece of paper with a fat-tipped marker and then place the fabric over the guide.

When the label is complete, press under the raw edges and attach to the lower-right corner of the back of the quilt with a blind hem stitch.

NATIVE RAINBOW

N ATIVE RAINBOW by Laurie Shifrin, 2000, Seattle, Washington, 61" x 68". Machine quilted by Sherry Rogers. Walk across the painted Southwestern desert with this Square in a Square earth-tone block. A cream background sets off the cobblestoned medallion from its triple inner border. The limitless combination of batiks in this diagonally set quilt makes it a timeless classic.

FINISHED QUILT SIZE

61" x 68"

MATERIALS

40"-wide fabric

- ½ yd. each of 10 earth-tone batiks for pieced blocks and border 2 squares (⅜ yd. each if using 16 or more batiks)
- ¾ yd. beige batik for side and corner triangles
- ⅞ yd. dark green batik for border 1 and border 3
- ½ yd. stripe batik for border 2
- 2 yds. swirly-print batik for border 4
- 4 yds. for backing (pieced horizontally)
- ⅔ yd. for binding
- 67" x 74" piece of batting

CUTTING

All measurements include ¼" seam allowances.

From the 10 earth-tone batiks, cut:

- 50 squares, 2½" x 2½", for pieced blocks (A)
- 48 squares, 2½" x 2½", for border 2
- 100 rectangles, each 2" x 9"; crosscut each rectangle into 3 rectangles, one 2" x 5½" (C, 100 total) and two 1½" x 2" (B, 200 total), keeping pieces from same fabric together

From the beige batik, cut:

- 5 squares, 8⅜" x 8⅜"; cut squares twice diagonally to yield 20 side triangles (you'll use 18)
- 2 squares, 4½" x 4½"; cut squares once diagonally to yield 4 corner triangles

From the dark green batik, cut:

- 2 strips, 1¾" x 38⅜", for border 1 top and bottom

- 3 strips, 1¾" x 40", for border 1 sides
- 6 strips, 2¼" x 40", for border 3

From the stripe batik, cut:

- 2 strips, 2½" x 21½", for border 2 sides
- 2 strips, 2½" x 18⅜", for border 2 top and bottom

From the swirly-print batik, cut:

- 4 strips along lengthwise grain, 8" wide by the length of the fabric, for border 4

From the fabric for binding, cut:

- 7 strips, 2½" x 40"

QUILT-TOP ASSEMBLY

1. Sew 2 different B rectangles together on their long sides. Repeat. Sew both units to opposite sides of an A square of a different fabric. Make 50 units.

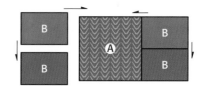

Make 50.

2. Sew a C rectangle to each side of the unit made in step 1, matching the fabric to the adjoining smaller B rectangles. Make 50 blocks in different fabric combinations.

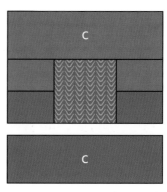

Make 50.

3. Arrange the blocks in diagonal rows, alternating the direction of the center seam of each block as shown. To achieve a well-balanced, scrappy look, distribute like fabrics and values evenly throughout the quilt top. Add the side and corner triangles. Referring to "Diagonally Set Quilts" (page 23), sew the blocks and triangles together in diagonal rows. Join the rows, adding the corner triangles last.

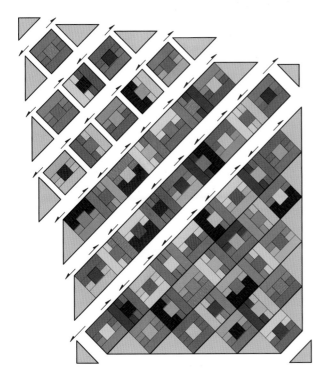

BORDER ASSEMBLY AND FINISHING

1. Sew 3 dark green 1¾" x 40" border 1 strips together end to end. From this long strip, cut 2 pieces 43" long and sew these to opposite sides of the quilt top. Sew the dark green 1¾" x 38⅜" border 1 strips to the top and bottom edges.

2. For border 2, sew together 6 earth-tone batik 2½" squares. Make 8 strips total. Mix up the fabrics for a random look.

3. Sew a strip from step 2 to each end of each 2½"-wide border 2 strip.

Make 4.

4. Sew the longer border 2 strips to the sides of the quilt top. Sew the remaining border 2 strips to the top and bottom edges.

5. Referring to "Straight Cut Borders" (page 24), measure, trim, and sew border 3 to the quilt top. Repeat with border 4.

6. Referring to "Finishing" (page 27), layer the quilt top with batting and backing; baste. Quilt as desired. Bind the edges; add a label.

> TIP: For a smaller quilt, leave off the final border.

TRIP SQUARED

TRIP SQUARED designed by Laurie Shifrin, pieced and machine quilted by Diane Roubal, 2000, Seattle, Washington, 51½" x 51½". If you've ever tried the Trip around the World pattern, you know how easy and rewarding it is to piece. This quilt goes to the next dimension by setting a small trip on point inside a larger trip. You can feature a collection of batiks in one color range, or you can make the transition from one trip to the other with a dramatic choice of color.

FINISHED QUILT SIZE

51½" x 51½"

MATERIALS

40"-wide fabric

- **From dark to light (inner trip, from center out):**
  - Fabric 1: ⅞ yd. darkest purple batik for inner and outer trips, inner trip side and corner triangles
  - Fabric 2: 1 yd. dark purple-print batik
  - Fabric 3: ⅞ yd. dark purple-and-burgundy batik for inner and outer trips
  - Fabric 4: ¾ yd. purple filigree-print batik for inner and outer trips
  - Fabric 5: ¾ yd. burgundy chevron-print batik for inner and outer trips
  - Fabric 6: ⅜ yd. burgundy leaf-print batik for inner and outer trips
  - Fabric 7: ½ yd. burgundy feather-print batik for inner and outer trips
  - Fabric 8: ⅜ yd. pink batik for inner trip
  - Fabric 9: ¾ yd. green batik for inner border and outer-trip side and corner triangles
- 3⅜ yds. for backing
- ⅝ yd. for binding
- 57" x 57" piece of batting

CUTTING

All measurements include ¼" seam allowances.

From fabrics 1 through 8, cut strips across fabric width for the inner and outer trips:

	Inner trip 2⅝"-wide strips	Outer trip 3½"-wide strips
Fabric 1	—	6
Fabric 2	1	6
Fabric 3	1	5
Fabric 4	1	4
Fabric 5	2	3
Fabric 6	2	2
Fabric 7	2	1
Fabric 8	2	—

From fabric 1, also cut:

- 1 square, 2⅝" x 2⅝"

From fabric 2, also cut:

- 1 strip, 4¼" x 40"; crosscut strip into 7 squares, 4¼" x 4¼". Cut squares twice diagonally to yield 28 side triangles (A). From the remainder of the strip, cut 2 squares, 2⅜" x 2⅜". Cut squares once diagonally to yield 4 corner triangles (B).

From fabric 8, also cut:

- 4 squares, 2⅝" x 2⅝"

From fabric 9, cut:

- 2 strips, 2" x 24½"
- 2 strips, 2" x 27½"
- 2 strips, 5½" x 40"; crosscut strips into a total of 11 squares, 5½" x 5½". Cut squares twice diagonally to yield 44 side triangles (C). From remainder of strips, cut 2 squares, 3⅞" x 3⅞". Cut squares once diagonally to yield 4 corner triangles (D).

From the fabric for binding, cut:

- 6 strips, 2½" x 40"

QUILT-TOP ASSEMBLY AND FINISHING

1. For the inner trip, cut each 2⅝" x 40" strip into 3 pieces, approximately 13" long. Sew the strips together to make one each of the following strip sets, keeping one end even. Crosscut the strip sets into 2⅝"-wide segments as indicated.

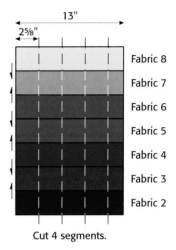

13"
2⅝"

Fabric 8
Fabric 7
Fabric 6
Fabric 5
Fabric 4
Fabric 3
Fabric 2

Cut 4 segments.

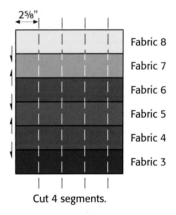

2⅝"

Fabric 8
Fabric 7
Fabric 6
Fabric 5
Fabric 4
Fabric 3

Cut 4 segments.

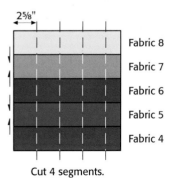

2⅝"

Fabric 8
Fabric 7
Fabric 6
Fabric 5
Fabric 4

Cut 4 segments.

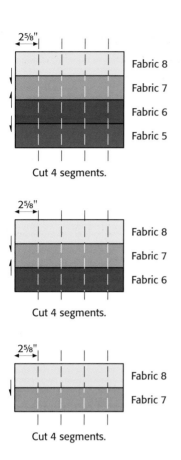

2⅝"

Fabric 8
Fabric 7
Fabric 6
Fabric 5

Cut 4 segments.

2⅝"

Fabric 8
Fabric 7
Fabric 6

Cut 4 segments.

2⅝"

Fabric 8
Fabric 7

Cut 4 segments.

TIP: If you sew the strips together so that the new strip you're adding is always on top, the top edge of the strip unit will remain even.

2. Arrange the segments as shown, adding a fabric 8 square to each end. Sew an A side triangle to the top of each fabric 8 square except for on the middle segment. Sew an A triangle to the remaining side of the fabric 8 square at each end. Join the rows to make a triangle section. Make 2 triangle sections total. Press the seams of one section to the right and the seams of the other section to the left.

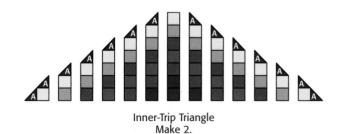

Inner-Trip Triangle
Make 2.

3. Sew both remaining 8-7-6-5-4-3-2 segments to opposite sides of a fabric 1 square to make the center row of the inner trip. Press the seams in one direction.

Inner-Trip Center Row
Make 1.

4. Sew a triangle section to the center row. Rotate the center row as needed so the seams butt. Sew the remaining triangle section to the other side of the center row. Sew a fabric 2 B triangle to each corner.

5. Sew the 2" x 24½" fabric 9 border strips to opposite sides of the quilt top. Sew the 2" x 27½" fabric 9 border strips to the top and bottom edges.

6. For the outer trip, sew the 3½" x 40" strips together to make one each of the following strip sets, keeping one end even. Crosscut the strip sets into 3½"-wide segments as indicated.

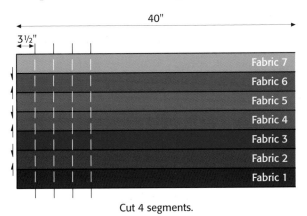

Cut 4 segments.

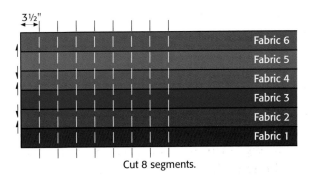

Cut 8 segments.

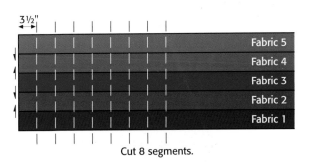

Cut 8 segments.

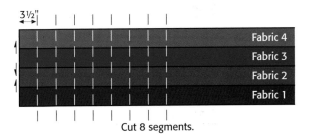

Cut 8 segments.

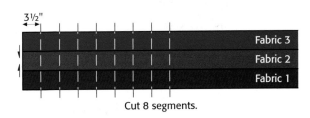

Cut 8 segments.

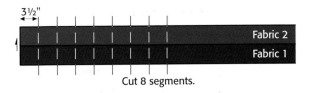

Cut 8 segments.

7. Using a seam ripper, remove the fabric 2 squares from half of the fabric 2-1 segments. Discard the fabric 2 squares.

8. Arrange the segments as shown to make 2 each of sections X and Y. Add a fabric 1 square to both ends of each section Y. Add a fabric 9 C triangle to the top of each fabric 1 square except for on the center strips, and at each end. Join the rows to complete each section.

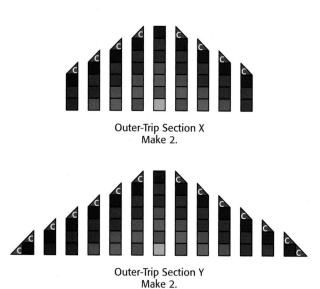

Outer-Trip Section X
Make 2.

Outer-Trip Section Y
Make 2.

9. Pin and sew the X sections to opposite sides of the quilt top, easing as necessary. Pin and sew the Y sections to the remaining sides of the quilt top, easing as necessary. Sew the fabric 9 D triangles to each corner of the quilt top.

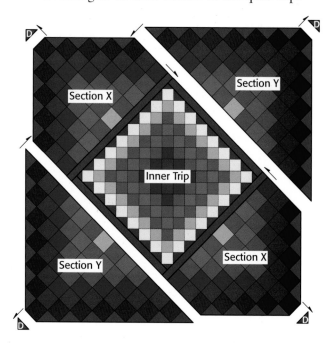

10. Referring to "Finishing" (page 127), layer the quilt top with batting and backing; baste. Quilt as desired. Bind the edges; add a label.

JEWELS AND JUMBLES

JEWELS AND JUMBLES by Laurie Shifrin, 2000, Seattle, Washington, 54¾" x 68¾". Machine quilted by Gretchen Engle. The sashing and inner border of small quarter-square triangles presents a dazzling framework for the jewel-toned stars. This quilt will sparkle whether scrappy or not.

FINISHED QUILT SIZE

54¾" x 68¾"

MATERIALS

40"-wide fabric

- ½ yd. each of 12 medium blue, purple, and green batiks for stars and sashing strips (⅜ yd. each if using 24 fabrics)
- 1⅜ yds. light green batik for star background
- ⅜ yd. dark purple for inner border
- 1⅜ yds. multicolored print batik for outer border
- 3½ yds. for backing (pieced horizontally)
- ¾ yd. for binding
- 60" x 74" piece of batting

CUTTING

All measurements include ¼" seam allowances.

From the assorted blue, purple, and green batiks, cut:

- 12 squares, 4½" x 4½" (D)
- 24 squares, 4⅞" x 4⅞". Select 2 matching squares for each star. Cut squares once diagonally to yield 48 half-square triangles (C) (4 per star).
- 12 squares, 5¼" x 5¼". Cut squares twice diagonally to yield 48 triangles (A) (4 per star).
- 206 squares, 3¼" x 3¼" (F) for sashing.

From the light green batik, cut:

- 6 strips, 4½" x 40"; crosscut strips into a total of 48 squares, 4½" x 4½" (E).
- 2 strips, 5¼" x 40"; crosscut strips into a total of 12 squares, 5¼" x 5¼". Cut squares twice diagonally to yield 48 triangles (B).

From the dark purple batik, cut:

- 8 strips, 1⅛" x 40"

From the multicolored print batik, cut:

- 8 strips, 5" x 40"

From the fabric for binding, cut:

- 7 strips, 2½" x 40"

QUILT-TOP ASSEMBLY

1. Sew together a blue, purple, or green A triangle, a light green B triangle, and a blue, purple, or green C triangle as shown. Make 4 identical units for each star (48 units total).

Make 4 identical units
for each star.

2. Sew together 4 matching units from step 1, a blue, purple, or green D square, and 4 light green E squares to make a Twisted Star block. Make 12 blocks.

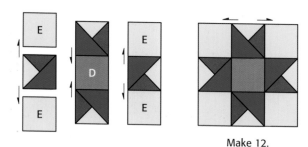

Make 12.

3. Referring to "Quarter-Square-Triangle Units" (page 20) and using the F squares, make 206 units. Mix fabrics randomly to create a scrappy look.

Make 206.

4. For vertical sashing strips, sew together 6 units from step 3. Make 16 strips total. For horizontal sashing strips, sew together 22 units from step 3. Make 5 strips total.

Make 16.

Make 5.

5. Arrange the 12 Twisted Star blocks as shown. Add vertical sashing strips between the blocks and at the ends of each row. Sew the blocks and sashing strips together. Join the rows with the horizontal sashing strips in between each row and at the top and bottom edges.

BORDER ASSEMBLY AND FINISHING

1. Sew together the 1⅛" x 40" inner-border strips end to end in pairs. Repeat for the 5" x 40" outer-border strips. Sew 1 inner-border strip to each outer-border strip. Press the seams toward the inner border on 2 of the strips and trim to 60" for the top and bottom borders. Press the seams toward the outer border on the 2 remaining strips for the side borders.

2. Referring to "Mitered Borders" (page 25), sew the borders to the quilt top and miter the corners.

3. Referring to "Finishing" (page 27), layer the quilt top with batting and backing; baste. Quilt as desired. Bind the edges; add a label.

MODERN MAYHEM

MODERN MAYHEM by Laurie Shifrin, 2000, Seattle, Washington, 49¼" x 63½". Squares and rectangles mingle together in this distinctive, elegant quilt. It's ideal for exhibiting the many batiks in your stash. Or try this quilt using just one printed batik for the larger squares while drawing out complementary colors in the rectangles and small squares.

Skill Level: Beginner □

FINISHED QUILT SIZE

49¼" x 63½"

MATERIALS

40"-wide fabric

- ½ yd. each of 10 assorted earth-tone batiks for piecing (⅜ yd. each if using 15 or more batiks)
- 3¼ yds. for backing (pieced horizontally)
- ⅝ yd. for binding
- 55" x 69" piece of batting

CUTTING

All measurements include ¼" seam allowances.

From the assorted earth-tone batiks, cut:
- 130 squares, 4" x 4" (A)
- 154 squares, 1¾" x 1¾" (B)
- 283 rectangles, 1¾" x 4" (C)

From the fabric for binding, cut:
- 6 strips, 2½" x 40"

TIP: This quilt is easy to make in any size. Simply add or subtract rows.

QUILT-TOP ASSEMBLY AND FINISHING

1. Arrange the large A squares, small B squares, and C rectangles as shown. To give the quilt a scrappy, random look, distribute similar fabrics evenly throughout the quilt top.

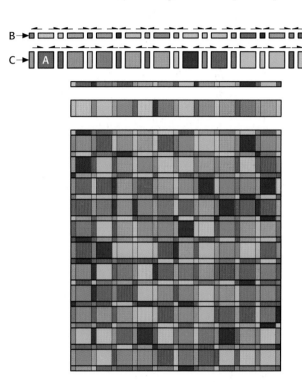

2. Sew the pieces together in rows. Join the rows.

3. Referring to "Finishing" (page 27), layer the quilt top with batting and backing; baste. Quilt as desired. Bind the edges; add a label.

WILD THING

WILD THING by Laurie Shifrin, 2000, Seattle, Washington, 66" x 78⅝". Machine quilted by Becky Krause. This quilt was inspired by Margy Duncan's "Gingersnap Nine Patch." It features Nine Patch blocks, Four Patch blocks, and plain squares in alternating rounds. For a blended look, use fabrics that are similar in color and texture. For distinct rows around the quilt, use fabrics that stand out on their own. Or try a little of both, which is what I did!

Skill Level: Beginner ▣

FINISHED QUILT SIZE

66" x 78⅝"

MATERIALS

40"-wide fabric

All measurements include ¼" seam allowances.

- From the center out:
  - Fabric 1: ¼ yd. for round 1 plain squares
  - Fabric 2a: ¼ yd. for round 2 Nine Patch blocks
  - Fabric 2b: ¼ yd. for round 2 Nine Patch blocks
  - Fabric 3: ½ yd. for round 3 plain squares
  - Fabric 4a: ⅜ yd. for round 4 Nine Patch blocks
  - Fabric 4b: ⅜ yd. for round 4 Nine Patch blocks
  - Fabric 5: ⅝ yd. for round 5 plain squares
  - Fabric 6a: ½ yd. for round 6 Four Patch blocks
  - Fabric 6b: ½ yd. for round 6 Four Patch blocks
  - Fabric 7: ¾ yd. for round 7 plain squares
  - Fabric 8a: ⅝ yd. for round 8 Four Patch blocks
  - Fabric 8b: ⅝ yd. for round 8 Four Patch blocks
  - Fabric 9: ¾ yd. for side and corner triangles
  - Fabric 10: 2⅛ yds. for border
- ¾ yd. for binding
- 5 yds. for backing (pieced vertically)
- 72" x 84" piece of batting

CUTTING

All measurements include ¼" seam allowances.

Cut strips for rounds 1–8 as follows across fabric width:

	Strip width	No. of strips	Crosscut strips into
Fabric 1	5"	1	3 squares, 5" x 5"
Fabric 2a	2"	3	—
Fabric 2b	2"	3	—
Fabric 3	5"	2	12 squares, 5" x 5"
Fabric 4a	2"	4	—
Fabric 4b	2"	5	—
Fabric 5	5"	3	20 squares, 5" x 5"
Fabric 6a	2¾"	4	—
Fabric 6b	2¾"	4	—
Fabric 7	5"	4	28 squares, 5" x 5"
Fabric 8a	2¾"	5	—
Fabric 8b	2¾"	5	—

From fabric 9, cut:

- 8 squares, 7⅝" x 7⅝". Cut squares twice diagonally to yield 32 side triangles.
- 2 squares, 4⅛" x 4⅛". Cut squares once diagonally to yield 4 corner triangles.

From fabric 10, cut:

- 4 strips along lengthwise grain, 7¾" wide by the length of the fabric

From the fabric for binding, cut:

- 8 strips, 2½" x 40"

QUILT-TOP ASSEMBLY

1. To make the Nine Patch blocks for round 2, sew fabric strips 2a and 2b together to make strip sets A and B. Crosscut A into 8 segments, each 2" wide. Crosscut B into 16 segments, also 2" wide. Sew an A segment between 2 B segments to make a Nine Patch block. Make 8 blocks.

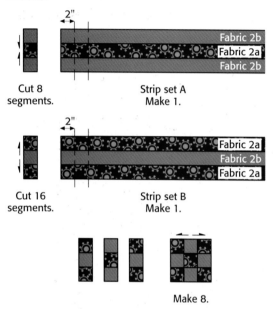

Cut 8 segments.

Strip set A
Make 1.

Cut 16 segments.

Strip set B
Make 1.

Make 8.

2. To make the Nine Patch blocks for round 4 sew fabric strips 4a and 4b together to make 1 strip set A and 2 strip sets B. Crosscut A into 16 segments, 2" wide, and B into 32 segments, 2" wide. Join as in step 1 to make 16 blocks.

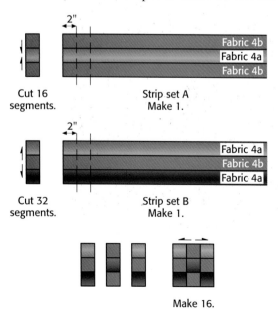

Cut 16 segments.

Strip set A
Make 1.

Cut 32 segments.

Strip set B
Make 1.

Make 16.

3. To make the Four Patch blocks for round 6, sew fabric strips 6a and 6b together in pairs to make 4 strip sets. Crosscut the strip sets into 48 segments, 2¾" wide. Sew 2 segments together, rotating one of them, to make a Four Patch block. Make 24 blocks.

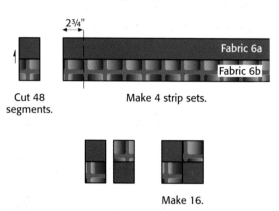

Cut 48 segments.

Make 4 strip sets.

Make 16.

4. To make the Four Patch blocks for round 8, sew strips 8a and 8b together in pairs to make 5 strip sets. Crosscut them into 64 segments, 2¾" wide. Join as in step 3 to make 32 blocks.

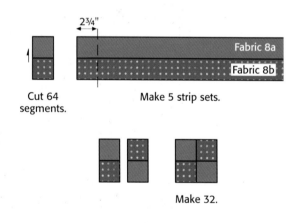

Cut 64 segments.

Make 5 strip sets.

Make 32.

TIP: You can easily change the quilt size by adding or taking away rounds.

5. Arrange the plain squares, Nine Patch blocks, and Four Patch blocks in diagonal rows as shown. Add the side and corner triangles. Referring to "Diagonally Set Quilts" (page 23), sew the squares, blocks, and triangles together in diagonal rows. Join the rows, adding the corner triangles last.

BORDER ASSEMBLY AND FINISHING

1. Referring to "Straight-Cut Borders" (page 24), measure, trim, and sew the fabric 10 border strips to the quilt top.

2. Referring to "Finishing" (page 27), layer the quilt top with batting and backing; baste. Quilt as desired. Bind the edges; add a label.

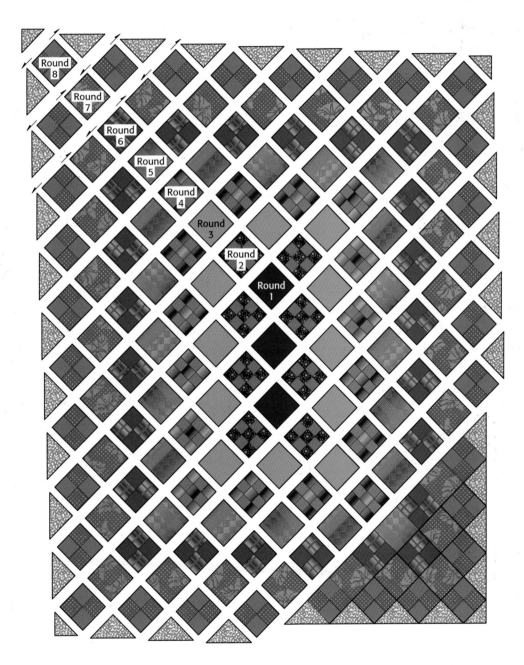

BEHIND THE SHADOWS

BEHIND THE SHADOWS by Laurie Shifrin, 2000, Seattle, Washington, 66½" x 84½". Machine quilted by Becky Krause. This quilt uses simple shapes and only four fabrics to create a stunning illusion. The small squares form a chain that appear as a shadow behind the larger triangle pattern.

Skill Level: Beginner □

FINISHED QUILT SIZE
66½" x 84½"

MATERIALS
40"-wide fabric

- 2⅜ yds. gold batik for Shadow blocks and middle border
- ⅝ yd. brown batik for Shadow blocks
- 1¼ yds. black batik for Shadow blocks and inner border
- 3¾ yds. black-and-gold print batik for Shadow blocks and outer border
- 5¼ yds. for backing (pieced vertically)
- ¾ yd. for binding
- 72" x 90" piece of batting

CUTTING

All measurements include ¼" seam allowances.

From the gold batik, cut:
- 5 strips, 2" x 40"
- 6 strips, 3½" x 40"
- 7 strips, 5⅜" x 40"
- 8 strips, 1¼" x 40"

From the brown batik, cut:
- 8 strips, 2" x 40"

From the black batik, cut:
- 8 strips, 2" x 40"
- 8 strips, 2¼" x 40"

From the black-and-gold batik print, cut:
- Along the crosswise grain:
  - 7 strips, 5⅜" x 40"
- Along the lengthwise grain:
  - 3 strips, 2" x 84". Cut strips in half so they are 42" long.
  - 3 strips, 3½" x 84". Cut strips in half so they are 42" long.
  - 4 strips, 4¾" x 84"

From the fabric for the binding, cut:
- 8 strips, 2½" x 40"

QUILT-TOP ASSEMBLY

1. To make the four-patch units, sew gold and brown 2" strips together in pairs to make 5 strip sets. Crosscut the strip sets into 96 segments, each 2" wide. Sew 2 segments together, rotating one of them, to make a four-patch unit. Make 48 gold-and-brown units.

Make 5 strip sets.
Cut 96 segments.

Make 48.

Repeat, joining the black and black-and-gold 2" strips, to make 48 units.

Make 5 strip sets.
Cut 96 segments.

Make 48.

2. Sew brown 2" strips and gold 3½" strips together in pairs to make 3 strip sets. Crosscut the strip sets into 48 segments, each 2" wide.

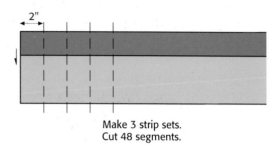

Make 3 strip sets.
Cut 48 segments.

Repeat with black 2" strips and black-and-gold 3½" strips.

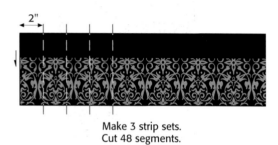

Make 3 strip sets.
Cut 48 segments.

3. Cut the remaining gold 3½" strips into 48 segments, each 2" wide. Also cut the remaining black-and-gold 3½" strips into 48 segments, 2" wide.

4. To each gold-and-brown four-patch unit, sew a gold 3½" rectangle and a gold-and-brown segment from step 2. Make 48 units. To each four-patch unit made of black and black-and-gold, sew a 3½" black-and-gold rectangle and a coordinating segment from step 2. Make 48 units.

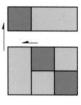

Make 48.   Make 48.

5. Referring to "Multiple Half-Square-Triangle Units" (page 21), use the gold 5⅜" strips and the black-and-gold 5⅜" strips to make 96 half-square-triangle units.

Make 96.

6. Sew together 2 triangle units and 2 square units to make a Shadow block. Make 48 blocks.

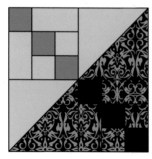

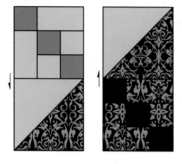

Make 48.

7. Arrange the blocks as shown, rotating as needed to establish the design. Sew the blocks together in rows. Join the rows.

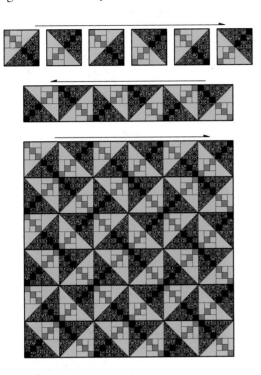

BORDER ASSEMBLY AND FINISHING

1. Sew the 2¼" x 40" black inner-border strips together end to end in pairs. Referring to "Straight-Cut Borders" (page 24), measure, trim, and sew the inner-border strips to the quilt top.

2. To make the mock-piping middle border, sew the gold 1¼" x 40" strips together in pairs. Fold in half, wrong side in, and press.

3. Pin 1 strip to each side edge of the quilt top, aligning the raw edges of the piping and inner border; stitch. Press flat; don't press the seam allowance to one side. Trim the ends even with quilt top. Repeat to join the remaining mock piping to the top and bottom edges.

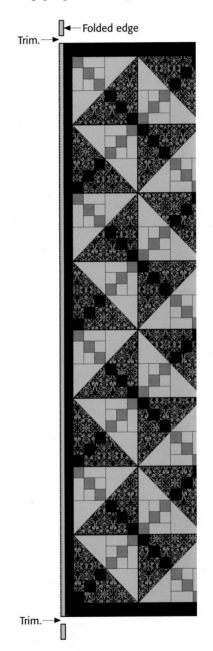

4. Referring to "Straight-Cut Borders" (page 24), measure, trim, and sew the 4¾" x 84" outer-border strips to the quilt top.

5. Referring to "Finishing" (page 27), layer the quilt top with batting and backing; baste. Quilt as desired. Bind edges and add a label.

TRIP TO INDONESIA

TRIP TO INDONESIA by Laurie Shifrin, 2000, Seattle, Washington, 38" x 38". Show off your favorite printed batik in this intriguing but simple wall hanging. Eight solid-looking batiks, hand-dyed fabrics, or solids draw out the colors from the featured batik fabric.

FINISHED QUILT SIZE

38" x 38"

MATERIALS

40"-wide fabric

- ⅓ yd. each of 8 solid, hand-dyed, or solid-looking fabrics for piecing
- 1¼ yds. batik print for plain squares and border
- 1¾ yds. for backing
- ½ yd. for binding
- 45" x 45" piece of batting

CUTTING

All measurements include ¼" seam allowances.

From the batik print, cut:
- 1 strip, 8" x 40"; crosscut strip into 4 squares, 8" x 8"
- 4 strips, 5" x 40"

Arrange the 8 "solid" fabrics in a pleasing order, for example, from light to dark or moving through the color spectrum; in my quilt, light green is fabric 1 and light purple is fabric 8. For future reference, cut a small piece from the selvage of each fabric, tape the pieces in order to a piece of paper, and number them 1 through 8. Cut the fabrics, parallel to the selvage, into 2"-wide strips as indicated.

Trim selvage.

	2"-wide strips
Fabric 1	3
Fabric 2	6
Fabric 3	10
Fabric 4	12
Fabric 5	14
Fabric 6	15
Fabric 7	17
Fabric 8	12

From fabric for binding, cut:
- 5 strips, 2½" x 40"

QUILT-TOP ASSEMBLY

1. Sew 2" x 12" strips together as shown. Make 7 strip sets for Block A, 2 for Block B, 3 for Block C, and 3 for Block D. Keep one edge of each set even. Press the seams toward the even-numbered fabrics. Crosscut each strip set into 2"-wide segments as indicated.

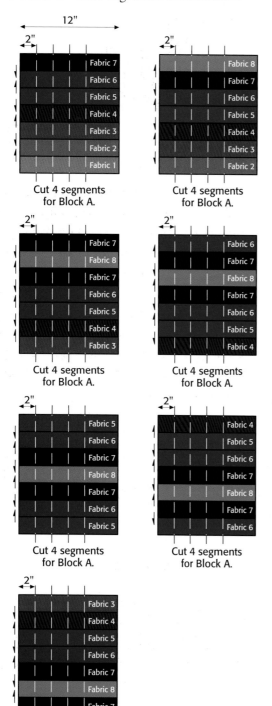

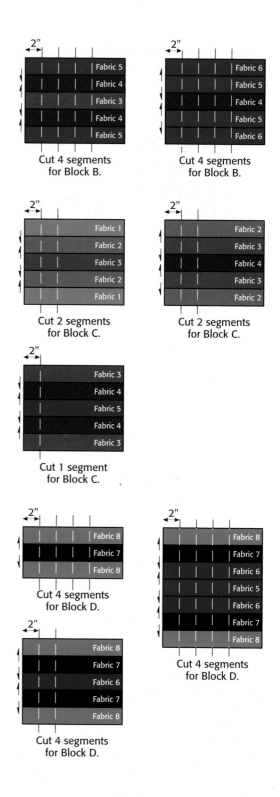

TIP: If you sew the strips together so that the new strip you're adding is always on top, the top edge of the strip unit will remain even.

2. Arrange and sew the segments together as shown. Make 4 of Block A, 4 of Block B, 1 of Block C, and 4 of Block D.

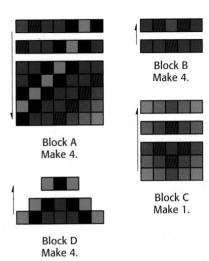

Block B
Make 4.

Block A
Make 4.

Block C
Make 1.

Block D
Make 4.

3. Sew each B block to an 8" batik square.

Make 4.

4. Arrange the blocks and pieced units as shown, paying careful attention to the orientation of the A blocks. Sew the blocks into rows. Join the rows to complete the center of the quilt top.

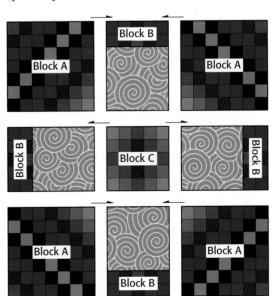

BORDER ASSEMBLY AND FINISHING

1. Trim the stepped sides of each D block through the fabric 8 squares, leaving a ¼" seam allowance as shown.

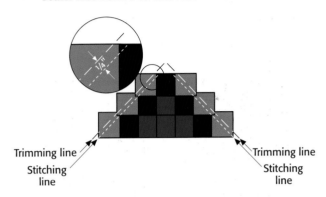

Trimming line
Stitching line

Trimming line
Stitching line

2. Fold a 5" x 40" batik-print outer-border strip in half and press the fold line with an iron. Unfold the strip. Align the ruler's 45° line on the strip's cut edge so that the edge of the ruler intersects the fold line as shown. Rotary cut along the edge of the ruler. Repeat to cut a second outer-border strip. To cut the remaining 2 strips, turn the ruler and align the 45° line facing the other direction (so the angled cut is reversed). Mark the right side of each cut piece with a pin.

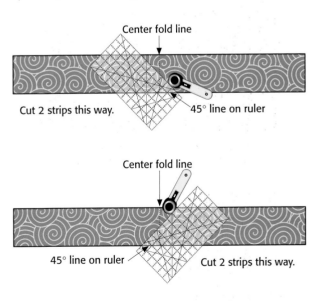

Center fold line

Cut 2 strips this way.

45° line on ruler

Center fold line

45° line on ruler

Cut 2 strips this way.

3. Sew a piece cut in step 2 to the diagonal side of a D block. Add another piece to the opposite diagonal side of the D block. Repeat with remaining pieces and D blocks to make 4 borders.

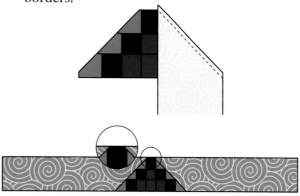

Make 4.

4. Referring to "Mitered Borders" (page 25), sew the borders to the center of the quilt top; match the seams of the squares and miter the corners.

5. Referring to "Finishing" (page 27), layer the quilt top with batting and backing; baste. Quilt as desired. Bind the edges; add a label.

EYE OF THE NEEDLE

LYE OF THE NEEDLE by Laurie Shifrin, 2000, Seattle, Washington, 54¾" x 72¼". Machine quilted by Becky Krause. Take the Log Cabin traditional block, throw in a twist, and you have a unique variation on a time-tested favorite. The small center square unfolds into a concentric diamond that comes alive through patterned batiks. Striking color contrasts make this a satisfying pattern in any palette.

FINISHED QUILT SIZE

54¾" x 72¼"

MATERIALS

40"-wide fabric

- From the center out:
  - Fabric 1: ⅛ yd. medium purple solid batik for center square
  - Fabric 2: ¾ yd. light chartreuse-print batik for center block and inner border
  - Fabric 3: ¼ yd. dark purple solid batik for small squares
  - Fabric 4: ⅝ yd. chartreuse-print batik for blocks
  - Fabric 5: ⅓ yd. violet solid batik for small squares
  - Fabric 6: 1¾ yds. green-and-purple-print batik for blocks and middle and outer borders
  - Fabric 7: ⅜ yd. blue solid batik for small squares and borders
  - Fabric 8: 1¼ yds. turquoise-and-purple-print batik for blocks
  - Fabric 9: ⅜ yd. plum solid batik for small squares and borders
  - Fabric 10: ⅝ yd. purple-and-blue-print batik for blocks
  - Fabric 11: ⅓ yd. bright purple solid batik for small squares and border
  - Fabric 12: ⅓ yd. green-and-turquoise-print batik for blocks
- 3⅝ yds. for backing (pieced horizontally)
- ¾ yd. for binding
- 60" x 78" piece of batting

CUTTING

All measurements include ¼" seam allowances.

Cut strips as follows across the fabric width:

	2¼"-wide strips
Fabric 2	8
Fabric 3	2
Fabric 4	7
Fabric 5	3
Fabric 6	22
Fabric 7	4
Fabric 8	12
Fabric 9	4
Fabric 10	7
Fabric 11	3
Fabric 12	3

Cut the 2¼"-wide strips into the lengths and quantities indicated. Always start with the largest cut. Label the pieces A through J for easy reference.

	(A)	(B)	(C)	(D)	(E)	(F)	(G)	(H)	(I)	(J)
Strip Length	18"	16¼"	14½"	12¾"	11"	9¼"	7½"	5¾"	4"	2¼"
Fabric 2					4	6	12	12		6
Fabric 3										20
Fabric 4						4	4	20	4	16
Fabric 5										40
Fabric 6	4	4	4	4	4	36	26	12		24
Fabric 7										60
Fabric 8						2	16	22	16	20
Fabric 9										62
Fabric 10							12	12	12	12
Fabric 11										44
Fabric 12							4	4	4	4

From fabric 1, cut:

• 1 square, 2¼" x 2¼" (J)

From the fabric for binding, cut:

• 8 strips, 2½" x 40"

QUILT-TOP ASSEMBLY

1. Arrange and sew the pieces together as shown, pressing between each step in the direction of the arrows. Make 1 center block.

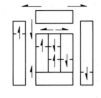

Make 1
with fabrics 1 and 2.

2. Arrange and sew the pieces together as shown, pressing between each step in the direction of the arrows. Make a total of 10 corner blocks.

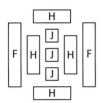

Make 4 with
fabrics 2, 3, and 4.   Make 4 with
fabrics 4, 5, and 6.

Make 2 with
fabrics 6, 7, and 8.

3. Arrange and sew the pieces together as shown, pressing between each step in the direction of the arrows. Make a total of 24 side blocks.

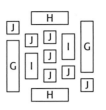

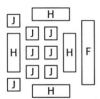

Make 4 with
fabrics 4, 5, and 6.   Make 8 with
fabrics 6, 7, and 8.

Make 8 with
fabrics 8, 9, and 10.   Make 4 with
fabrics 10, 11, and 12.

4. Arrange the 35 blocks as shown, paying careful attention to the color placement. Sew the blocks together in rows. Join the rows.

BORDER ASSEMBLY AND FINISHING

1. Arrange and sew together the remaining pieces as shown to make 2 each of borders A through F. Each piece in the diagram is labeled with a number, indicating the fabric, and a letter, indicating the strip length.

2. Sew the borders to the quilt top in the following order:

   A to the top and bottom
   B to the sides
   C to the top and bottom
   D to the sides
   E to the top and bottom
   F to the sides

3. Referring to "Finishing" (page 27), layer the quilt top with batting and backing; baste. Quilt as desired. Bind the edges; add a label.

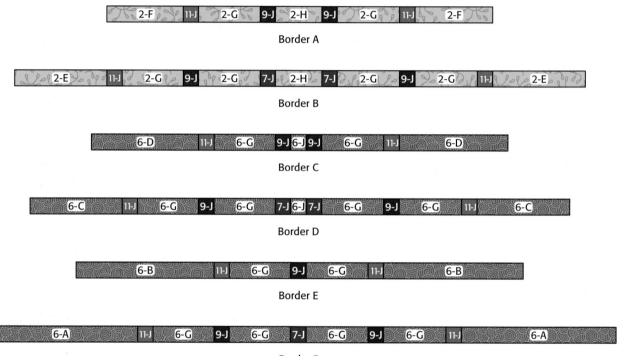

Border A

Border B

Border C

Border D

Border E

Border F

SNOWFLAKES AND WINTERBERRIES

SNOWFLAKES AND WINTERBERRIES by Laurie Shifrin, 2000, Seattle, Washington, 62½" x 62½". This charming quilt features a delicate snowflake fabric but can easily be adapted to your favorite novelty print. Using only two other fabrics, the design combines flying geese and square-in-a-square units in a striking arrangement. The border chain of squares goes together in a snap.

Skill Level: Intermediate

FINISHED QUILT SIZE

62½" x 62½"

MATERIALS

40"-wide fabric

- 1⅛ yds. white mottled batik for blocks
- 1⅜ yds. dark blue batik for blocks and inner borders
- 3⅞ yds. snowflake-print batik for blocks and borders
- 4 yds. for backing
- ⅝ yd. for binding
- 68" x 68" piece of batting

CUTTING

All measurements include ¼" seam allowances.

From the white mottled batik, cut:
- 2 strips, 2⅝" x 40"; crosscut strips into a total of 16 squares, 2⅝" x 2⅝" (A).
- 5 strips, 2⅜" x 40"; crosscut strips into a total of 80 squares, 2⅜" x 2⅜". Cut squares once diagonally to yield 160 triangles (B).
- 2 strips, 3½" x 40"; crosscut strips into a total of 20 squares, 3½" x 3½" (D).
- 1 strip, 2" x 40"; crosscut strip into 8 squares, 2" x 2" (J).

From the dark blue batik, cut:
- 2 strips, 2⅝" x 40"; crosscut strips into a total of 20 squares, 2⅝" x 2⅝" (A).
- 4 strips, 2⅜" x 40"; crosscut strips into a total of 64 squares, 2⅜" x 2⅜". Cut squares once diagonally to yield 128 triangles (B).

- 2 strips, 3½" x 40"; crosscut strips into a total of 16 squares, 3½" x 3½" (D).
- 1 strip, 2" x 40"; crosscut strip into 8 squares, 2" x 2" (J).
- 5 strips, 2⅝" x 40"; crosscut strips into a total of 68 squares, 2⅝" x 2⅝" (K).

From the snowflake-print batik, cut:
Along the lengthwise grain:
- 2 strips, 4½" wide by the full length of the fabric

Along the crosswise grain of the remaining fabric (approximately 31" wide):
- 3 strips, 4¼" x 31"; crosscut strips into a total of 18 squares, 4¼" x 4¼". Cut squares twice diagonally to yield 72 triangles (C).
- 3 strips, 2" x 31"; crosscut strips into a total of 36 squares, 2" x 2" (E).
- 3 strips, 2" x 31"; crosscut strips into a total of 36 rectangles, 3½" x 2" (G).
- 18 strips, 2½" x 31"; crosscut each strip into one 2½" x 12½" rectangle (H, 18 total), and one 2½" x 16½" rectangle (I, 18 total).
- 7 strips, 3" x 31"; crosscut strips into a total of 66 squares, 3" x 3". Cut squares once diagonally to yield 132 triangles (L).
- 1 strip, 2⅜" x 31"; crosscut strip into 4 squares, 2⅜" x 2⅜". Cut squares once diagonally to yield 8 triangles (M).
- 9 squares, 3½" x 3½" (F). If desired, fussy-cut the squares as I did to center a motif in each square.

From the fabric for binding, cut:
- 7 strips, 2½" x 40"

QUILT-TOP ASSEMBLY

1. Sew 2 white B triangles to opposite sides of a blue A square. Sew 2 white B triangles to the remaining sides of the square. Make 20 units. Repeat with blue B triangles and white A squares. Make 16 units.

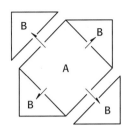

Make 20.   Make 16.

2. Sew 2 white B triangles to a snowflake-print D triangle. Make 40 units. Repeat with blue B triangles and snowflake-print C triangles. Make 32 units.

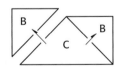

Make 40.   Make 32.

3. Arrange and sew together the units from steps 1 and 2 as shown. Make 5 white blocks and 4 blue blocks.

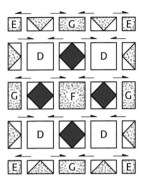 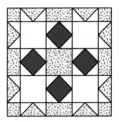

Make 5.

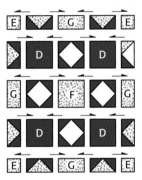 

Make 4.

4. Sew a snowflake-print H rectangle to each side of a block. Sew a snowflake-print I rectangle to the top and bottom edges.

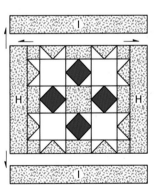

Make 5.

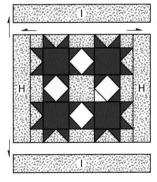

Make 4.

5. Arrange the white and blue blocks as shown. Using a sharp pencil, draw a diagonal line on the wrong side of 8 white 2" J squares and 8 blue 2" J squares. Referring to the diagram, pin the appropriate blue or white squares to the corner of the blocks, right sides together. Sew on each marked line and trim the seam allowance to ¼".

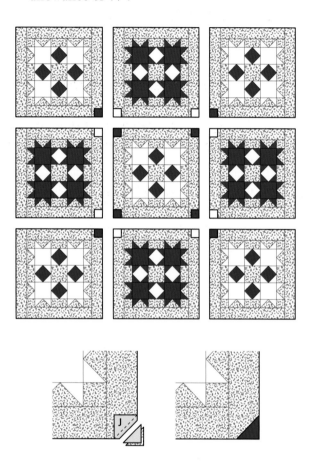

6. Sew the blocks together in rows. Press the seams toward the white blocks. Join the rows.

BORDER ASSEMBLY AND FINISHING

1. Sew the L and M snowflake-print triangles to the blue K squares as shown. Make 4 different units.

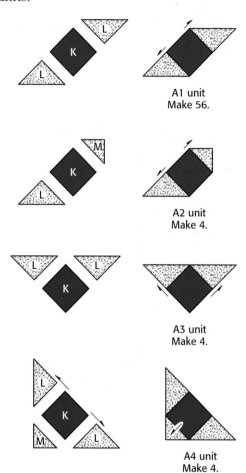

A1 unit
Make 56.

A2 unit
Make 4.

A3 unit
Make 4.

A4 unit
Make 4.

2. Sew 14 A1 units together. To complete the strip, add an A2 unit to the end on the right, and an A3 unit to the end on the left. Make 4 pieced border strips.

A3 unit

A2 unit

Make 4 border strips.

3. Pin a pieced border strip to the bottom of the quilt top, easing as necessary. The middle of the last L triangle on the left should be ¼" in from the left edge of the quilt top. With the border strip on top, sew the border starting at the edge of the quilt top and ending about 3" from the opposite end. You will complete this seam later. Press the seam toward the center of the quilt top.

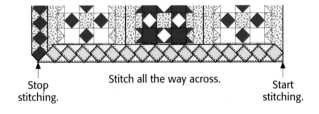

Stop stitching.   Start stitching.

4. Working counterclockwise, pin and sew the next border strip to the right side of the quilt top. Sew all the way from one edge to the other. Repeat to add border strips to the top and the left side. Press the seams toward the center of the quilt top.

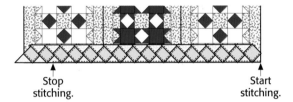

Stop stitching.   Stitch all the way across.   Start stitching.

5. Complete the seam from the first border strip. Sew an A4 unit to each corner of the quilt top.

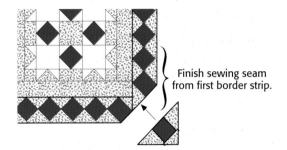

Finish sewing seam from first border strip.

6. Referring to "Straight-Cut Borders" (page 24), measure, trim, and sew the 4½"-wide snowflake-print outer-border strips to the quilt top. Press the seams toward the outer border.

7. Referring to "Finishing" (page 27), layer the quilt top with batting and backing; baste. Quilt as desired. Bind the edges and add a label.

EVENING CELESTIALS

EVENING CELESTIALS by Laurie Shifrin, 2000, Seattle, Washington, 43½" x 43½". The stark contrast of orange fabrics against a dark blue constellation print makes this wall hanging sparkle. The subtle burgundy inner border floats on a field of suspended stars and lights the way to a clear night of stargazing. I used four different oranges, but this design can also be made with just one.

Skill Level: Intermediate

FINISHED QUILT SIZE

43½" x 43½"

MATERIALS

40"-wide fabric

- ¼ yd. blue-and-orange leaf-print batik for center cross
- ¼ yd. each of 4 light orange-print batiks for squares (or ½ yd. of 1 light orange-print batik)
- ¼ yds. navy batik for star points
- ¼ yd. purple-and-orange-print batik for squares in center of stars
- ⅔ yd. multicolored batik for outer crosses and borders
- ¼ yd. blue-and-orange geometric-print batik for triangles and inner border
- ½ yd. burgundy batik for inner border
- 1⅞ yds. dark blue constellation-print batik for corners and outer border
- 3 yds. for backing
- ½ yd. for binding
- 49" x 49" piece of batting

CUTTING

All measurements include ¼" seam allowances.

From the blue-and-orange leaf-print batik, cut:

- 1 square, 5¼" x 5¼". Cut square twice diagonally to yield 4 triangles (A1)
- 1 square, 4½" x 4½" (B1)
- 4 rectangles, 2 ½" x 4½" (C1)

From each of the light orange-print batiks, cut:

- 4 squares, 3⁵⁄₁₆" x 3⁵⁄₁₆" (D, 16 total)
- 4 squares, 2½" x 2½" (E, 16 total)

From the navy batik, cut:

- 1 strip, 2⅞" x 40"; crosscut strip into 16 squares, 2⅞" x 2⅞". Cut squares once diagonally to yield 32 triangles (F).

From the purple-and-orange print, cut:

- 4 squares, 4½" x 4½" (G)

From the multicolored batik, cut:

- 4 squares, 5¼" x 5¼". Cut squares twice diagonally to yield 16 triangles (A2).
- 4 squares, 4½" x 4½" (B2)
- 2 strips, 2½" x 40"; crosscut strips into 16 rectangles, 2½" x 4½" (C2).

From the blue-and-orange geometric-print batik, cut:

- 4 squares, 5¼" x 5¼". Cut squares twice diagonally to yield 16 triangles (H).

From the burgundy batik, cut:

- 8 squares, 2⅞" x 2⅞". Cut squares once diagonally to yield 16 triangles (I).
- 8 squares, 2½" x 2½" (J)
- 8 rectangles 2½" x 10" (K)

From the dark blue constellation-print batik, cut:

- 2 squares, 5¼" x 5¼". Cut squares twice diagonally to yield 8 triangles (A3).
- 4 squares, 4½" x 4½" (B3)
- 8 rectangles, 2½" x 4½" (C3)
- 8 rectangles, 6" x 28" (L)

From the fabric for binding, cut:

- 5 strips, 2½" x 40"

QUILT-TOP ASSEMBLY

1. Arrange all the pieces for the center of the quilt top in groups 1 through 5 as shown. Sew the groups together in vertical rows.

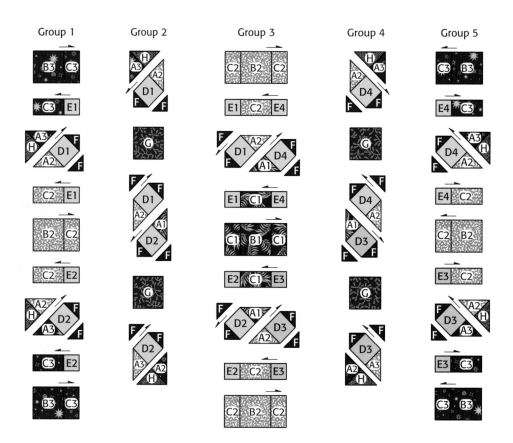

2. Sew the vertical rows together, matching the seams.

BORDER ASSEMBLY AND FINISHING

1. Assemble 4 inner-border strips as shown.

Make 4.

2. For the outer border, cut 4 of the 6" x 28" strips (L) at a 45° angle as shown to make left-facing strips. Cut the remaining 6" x 28" strips as shown to make 4 right-facing strips. Mark the right side of each piece with a pin.

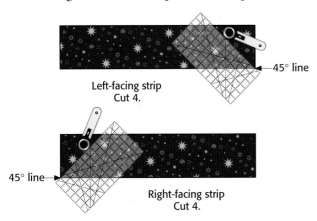

Left-facing strip
Cut 4.

45° line

45° line

Right-facing strip
Cut 4.

3. Sew the short side of an A2 triangle to a left-facing strip as shown, stopping ¼" from the end of the triangle and backstitching. Press the seam toward the triangle.

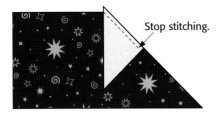

Stop stitching.

4. Sew a right-facing strip to the other side of the triangle, again stopping ¼" from the end and backstitching. Press the toward the triangle.

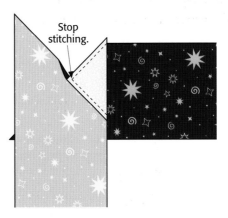

Stop stitching.

5. Fold the triangle in half, aligning the seams and the cut edges of the border strips. Mark a line from the tip of the triangle to the edge of the border strip. Pin along this line.

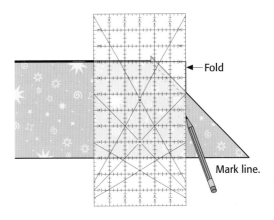

Fold

Mark line.

6. Beginning where the previous stitching ended, backstitch and then continue stitching along the marked line to the edge of the border strip. Unfold the strip and check that the border lies flat. Trim the seam allowance to ¼" and press the seam to one side. Repeat steps 3–6 to make 4 outer-border strips.

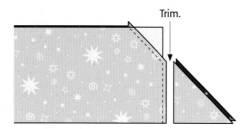

7. Sew 1 inner-border strip to each outer-border strip, matching the seams at the center triangle.

Make 4.

8. Referring to "Mitered Borders" (page 25), sew the borders to the quilt top; match the seams and miter the corners.

9. Referring to "Finishing" (page 27), layer the quilt top with batting and backing; baste. Quilt as desired. Bind the edges and add a label.

MYSTIQUE OF BALI

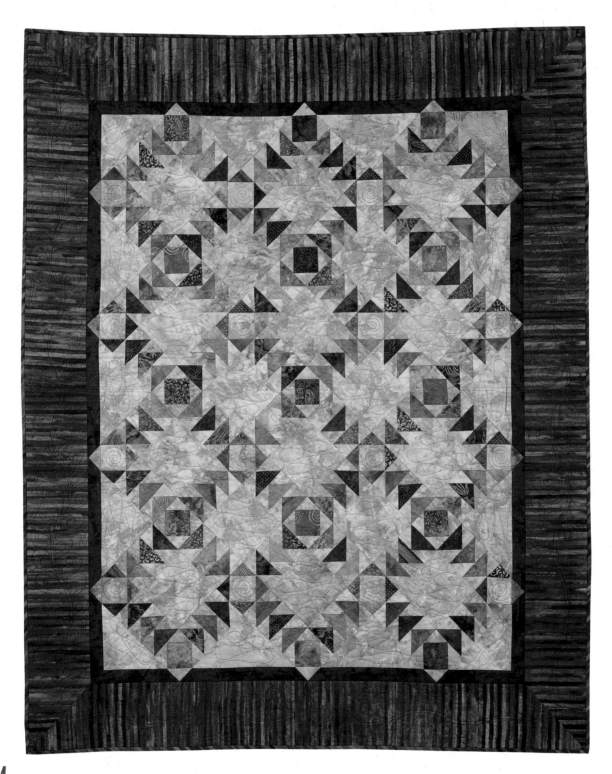

MYSTIQUE OF BALI by Laurie Shifrin, 2000, Seattle, Washington, 62½" x 76½". Machine quilted by Sherry Rogers. The circles of flying geese float over shades of rich turquoise. A closer look at the seemingly simple shapes in this quilt reveals countless secondary designs. The continuation of the "geese" into the first border is a pleasant surprise.

FINISHED QUILT SIZE

62½" x 76½"

MATERIALS

40"-wide fabric

- ⅜ yd. each of 8 or more assorted medium-to-dark blue and green batiks for piecing
- 3 yds. light turquoise batik for background
- ⅝ yd. dark batik for inner border
- 2 yds. striped batik for outer border
- 4⅞ yds. for backing (pieced vertically)
- ¾ yd. for binding
- 68" x 82" piece of batting

CUTTING

All measurements include ¼" seam allowances.

From the assorted blue and green batiks, cut:

- 36 squares, 5¼" x 5¼". Cut squares twice diagonally to yield 144 triangles (B).
- 15 squares, 3⁵⁄₁₆" x 3⁵⁄₁₆" (C).
- 32 squares, 2⅞" x 2⅞". Cut squares once diagonally to yield 64 triangles (A). Set aside 8 triangles from the lightest blue or green batiks for the inner border.

From the light turquoise batik, cut:

- 2 strips, 3⁵⁄₁₆" x 40"; crosscut strips into a total of 16 squares, 3⁵⁄₁₆" x 3⁵⁄₁₆" (C).
- 14 strips, 2⅞" x 40"; crosscut strips into a total of 174 squares, 2⅞" x 2⅞". Cut squares once diagonally to yield 348 triangles (A).
- 3 strips, 6½" x 40"; crosscut strips into a total of 18 squares, 6½" x 6½" (D).
- 1 strip, 12⁹⁄₁₆" x 40"; crosscut strip into 3 squares, 12⁹⁄₁₆" x 12⁹⁄₁₆". Cut squares twice diagonally to yield 12 setting triangles (E) (you'll use 10).

- 2 squares, 7¹⁵⁄₁₆" x 7¹⁵⁄₁₆". Cut squares once diagonally to yield 4 corner triangles (F).

From the dark batik, cut:

- 1 strip, 2⁵⁄₁₆" x 40"; crosscut strip into 14 squares, 2⁵⁄₁₆" x 2⁵⁄₁₆". Cut squares once diagonally to yield 28 triangles for inner border (G).
- 6 strips, 1¹⁵⁄₁₆" x 40"; crosscut strips into a total of 18 rectangles, 1¹⁵⁄₁₆" x 11¹³⁄₁₆" (H).

From the striped batik, cut:

- 8 strips, 7½" x 40"

From the fabric for binding, cut:

- 8 strips, 2½" x 40"

QUILT-TOP ASSEMBLY

1. Sew 2 background A triangles to the short sides of a blue or green B triangle. Make 144 units.

Make 144.

2. Choosing fabrics randomly, sew together 3 units from step 1, with the "geese" heading in the same direction. Make 48 units.

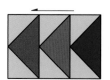

Make 48.

3. Sew 2 background A triangles to opposite sides of a blue or green C square. Sew 2 background A triangles to the remaining sides of the square. Make 9 units. Repeat with blue or green A triangles and background C squares. Make 8 units.

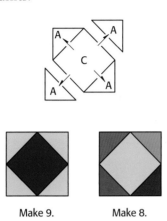

Make 9.   Make 8.

4. Sew 3 background A triangles to 3 sides of a blue or green C square. Make 6 units. Repeat with blue or green A triangles and background C squares. Make 8 units.

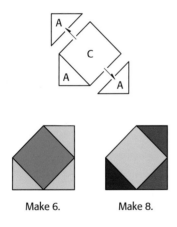

Make 6.   Make 8.

5. Arrange the units from steps 1 through 4 and the background D squares in diagonal rows as shown. Add the side and corner triangles. Referring to "Diagonally Set Quilts" (page 23), sew the units, squares, and triangles together in diagonal rows. Join the rows, adding the corner triangles last.

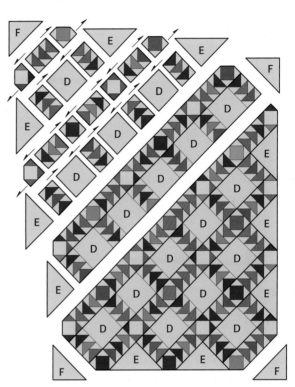

BORDER ASSEMBLY AND FINISHING

1. Sew 2 dark G triangles to each remaining A triangle. Make 14 units.

Make 6.   Make 8.

2. Sew together 3 background units from step 1 and 4 dark H rectangles to make the top and bottom inner borders. Sew together 4 blue or green units from step 1 and 5 dark H rectangles to make each side inner border.

Make 2 top and bottom border strips.

Make 2 side border strips.

3. Sew the outer-border strips together end to end in pairs. Center, pin, and sew each inner-border strip to an outer-border strip. Press the seams toward the outer-border strips.

Top and bottom borders

Side borders

4. Referring to "Mitered Borders" (page 25), sew the borders to the quilt top; match the A triangles in the borders to the C squares on the quilt top.

5. Referring to "Finishing" (page 27), layer the quilt top with batting and backing; baste. Quilt as desired. Bind the edges; add a label.

GLIMPSE OF THE PAST

GLIMPSE OF THE PAST by Laurie Shifrin, 2000, Seattle, Washington, 41" x 45½". This simple but striking wall hanging recalls the petroglyphs and other art forms of ancient cultures. The block—a simple square—has one pieced corner triangle. For an even scrappier look, increase the fabric selection for the squares and triangles. This is a great opportunity to use fat quarters.

Skill Level: Beginner 🔲

FINISHED QUILT SIZE

41" x 45½"

MATERIALS

40"-wide fabric

- ¼ yd. each of 8 medium earth-tone batiks for squares and accent triangles
- 1⅛ yd. light gray batik for background and sashing
- ⅓ yd. dark teal batik for inner border
- 1⅜ yds. medium print batik for outer border
- 2⅞ yds. for backing (pieced horizontally)
- ½ yd. for binding
- 47" x 51" piece of batting

> **TIP:** For a less scrappy quilt, try this quilt using only one fabric for the squares and another for the little triangles.

CUTTING

All measurements include ¼" seam allowances.

From each of the 8 medium earth tone batiks, cut:
- 4 squares, 3½" x 3½" (A, 32 total)
- 4 squares, 2" x 2" (B, 32 total)

From the light gray batik, cut:
- 2 strips, 5½" x 40"; crosscut strips into a total of 14 squares, 5½" x 5½". Cut squares twice diagonally to yield 56 triangles (C).
- 1 strip, 3" x 40"; crosscut strip into 8 squares, 3" x 3". Cut squares once diagonally to yield 16 triangles (D).
- 5 strips, 3" x 34½" (E)

From the dark teal batik, cut:
- 4 strips, 1½" x 40"

From the medium print batik, cut:
- 4 strips along lengthwise grain, 5" wide by the length of the fabric

From the fabric for binding, cut:
- 5 strips, 2½" x 40"

QUILT-TOP ASSEMBLY

1. Place a small B square in the top right corner of each large A square, right sides together. Mix up the fabrics randomly. Mark a diagonal line on the wrong side of the small square. Sew on the marked line. Trim the seam allowance to ¼" from the stitching line. Make 32 units.

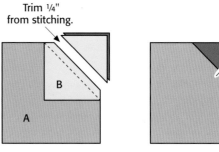

Trim ¼" from stitching.

Make 32.

2. Arrange the 32 squares as shown, mixing the order of the fabric for a pleasing, random look. Turn some squares so the triangles face different directions.

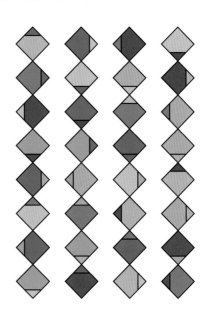

3. To the top square in each column, sew 1 light gray C triangle and 2 light gray D triangles as shown.

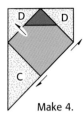

Make 4.

4. To the bottom square in each column, sew 1 light gray C triangle and 2 light gray D triangles as shown.

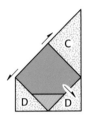

Make 4.

5. To the remaining squares in each column, sew 2 light gray C triangles as shown.

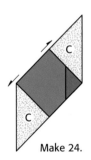

Make 24.

6. Sew the units in each column together. Press the seams toward the top of the column.

Make 4.

7. Fold each pieced column and sashing strip (E) in half; mark midpoint with pin. Matching the midpoints, pin and sew the sashing strips and pieced columns together; begin and end with a sashing strip. Press seams toward the sashing strips.

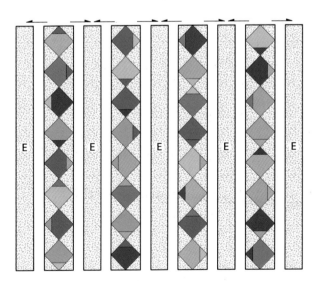

BORDER ASSEMBLY AND FINISHING

1. Sew one 1½" x 40" inner-border strip to each 5" outer-border strip. Press the seams toward the inner border. Referring to "Straight-Cut Borders" (page 24), measure, trim, and sew the borders to the quilt top.

2. Referring to "Finishing" (page 27), layer the quilt top with batting and backing; baste. Quilt as desired. Bind the edges; add a label.

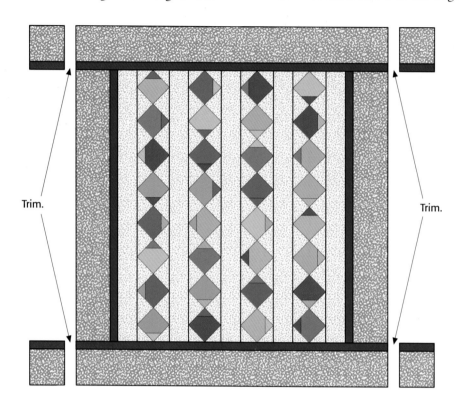

Trim.   Trim.

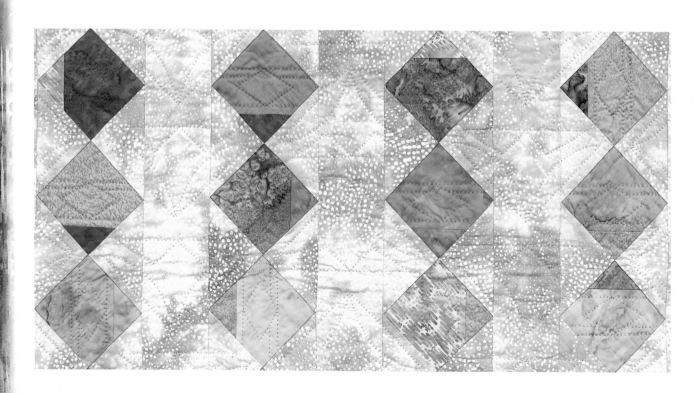

FIRE DANCE

F IRE DANCE by Laurie Shifrin, 2000, Seattle, Washington, 82" x 82". Machine quilted by Barbara Dau. Large center squares show off a favorite batik in this brilliant variation on the Irish Chain. This version goes one step further by incorporating triangles into the chains. The artistic element adds energy to a favorite heirloom design.

FINISHED QUILT SIZE

82" x 82"

MATERIALS

40"-wide fabric

- 1½ yds. yellow-and-peach-print batik for triangle chain and border triangles
- 3¾ yds. dark purple-print batik for triangle chain and borders
- 1 yd. yellow batik for inside chain
- 2¼ yds. orange-and-purple mottled batik for large blocks and border triangles
- 7⅝ yds. for backing
- ⅞ yd. for binding
- 88" x 88" piece of batting

CUTTING

All measurements include ¼" seam allowances.

From the yellow-and-peach-print batik, cut:
- 10 strips, 3⅜" x 40" (B1)
- 2 strips, 3¾" x 40" (C1)

From the dark purple-print batik, cut:
- 10 strips, 3⅜" x 40" (B2)
- 2 strips, 3¾" x 40" (C2)
- 4 strips, 3" x 40"; crosscut strips into a total of 8 rectangles, 3" x 18" (G)
- 4 strips, 5" x 23" (H)
- 4 strips, 5" x 27½" (I)
- 1 strip, 27½" x 40"; crosscut strip into 4 rectangles, 10" x 27½" (J)

From the yellow batik, cut:
- 10 strips, 3" x 40"; crosscut strips into a total of 125 squares, 3" x 3" (A)

From the orange-and-purple mottled batik, cut:
- 9 strips, 3" x 40"; crosscut 4 strips into a total of 52 squares, 3" x 3" (D). Crosscut remaining 5 strips into a total of 24 rectangles, 3" x 8" (E).
- 4 strips, 8" x 40"; crosscut strips into a total of 12 rectangles, 8" x 13" (F).
- 3 strips, 3⅜" x 40" (B3)

From the fabric for binding, cut:
- 9 strips, 2½" x 40"

QUILT-TOP ASSEMBLY

1. Referring to "Multiple Half-Square-Triangle Units" (page 21) and using 7 yellow-and-peach B1 strips and 7 dark purple B2 strips, make 152 B units.

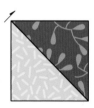

B unit
Make 152.

2. Referring to "Multiple Quarter-Square-Triangle Units" (page 21) and using 2 yellow-and-peach C1 strips and 2 dark purple C2 strips, make 52 quarter-square-triangle units.

Make 52.

3. Cut the remaining 3 dark purple B1 strips into 26 squares, 3⅜" x 3⅜". Cut squares once diagonally to yield 52 triangles. Sew each triangle to a unit made in step 2 to make 52 C units.

C unit
Make 52.

4. Arrange 9 yellow A squares, 8 B units, 4 C units, and 4 orange-and-purple D squares as shown. Sew the units together in rows. Join the rows to complete Block 1. Make 13 blocks.

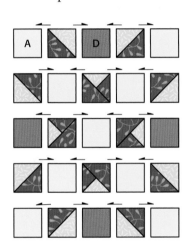

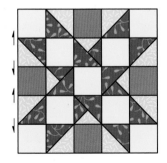

Block 1
Make 13.

5. Arrange 4 B units, 2 orange-and-purple E rectangles, and 1 orange-and-purple F rectangle as shown. Sew the units together in rows. Join the rows to complete Block 2. Make 12 blocks.

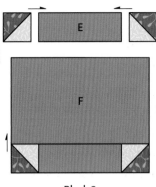

Block 2
Make 12.

6. Arrange Blocks 1 and 2 as shown, alternating the blocks from row to row. Sew the blocks together in rows. Join the rows.

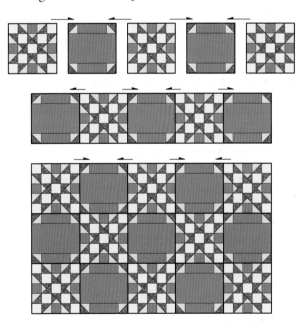

BORDER ASSEMBLY AND FINISHING

1. Referring to "Multiple Half-Square-Triangle Units" (page 21) and using 3 yellow-and-peach B1 strips and 3 orange-and-purple B3 strips, make 64 half-square-triangle units.

2. Sew together 8 half-square-triangle units into a strip. Make 8 strips.

Make 8.

3. Sew a dark purple G rectangle to the bottom edge of a triangle strip from step 2, stitching from the right-hand edge to about 2" from the left edge. Sew a dark purple H rectangle to the top of the strip, stitching from the right-hand edge to about 2" from the left edge. Make 4 left border units.

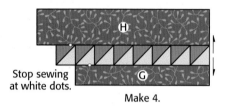

Stop sewing at white dots.

Make 4.

4. Sew a yellow A square to one end of each remaining triangle strip and dark purple G rectangle. Sew a G rectangle to the bottom edge of a triangle strip, stitching from the left-hand edge to about 2" from the right edge. Sew a dark purple I rectangle to the top of the triangle strip, stitching from the left-hand edge to about 2" from the right edge. Make 4 right border units.

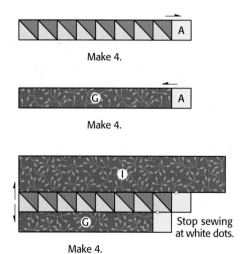

Make 4.

Make 4.

Stop sewing at white dots.

Make 4.

5. Sew a dark purple J rectangle between a left border unit and a right border unit. Make 4 border strips.

6. Mark 2½" from the triangle units in Block 2 on each side of the quilt top edge. Pin 1 border strip to one side of the quilt top, matching the seams on the border to these marks. With the border on top, sew from the beginning of the border strip to about 2" from the end. Repeat for all 4 borders.

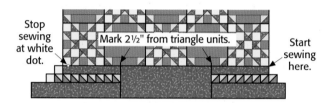

Stop sewing at white dot.

Mark 2½" from triangle units.

Start sewing here.

7. Finish sewing the segments of the border in numerical order as shown.

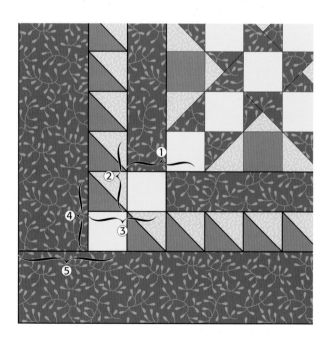

8. Referring to "Finishing" (page 27), layer the quilt top with batting and backing; baste. Quilt as desired. Bind the edges; add a label.

SPINNING DREAMS

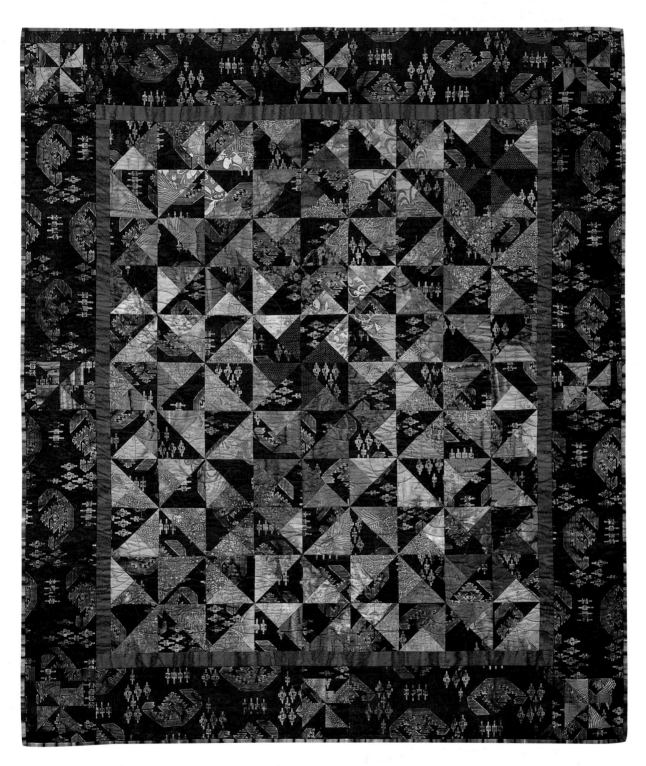

SPINNING DREAMS by Laurie Shifrin, 2000, Seattle, Washington, 63½" x 73½". Machine quilted by Gretchen Engle. Pinwheels and more pinwheels make this quilt a collage to explore. The smaller pinwheels could also be made from solid, marbled, or hand-dyed fabrics. Notice the subtle pinwheels placed in the border.

FINISHED QUILT SIZE

63½" x 73½"

MATERIALS

40"-wide fabric

- ⅜ yd. each of 8 or more assorted batiks for small pinwheels
- 4½ yds. dark theme-print batik for large pinwheels and borders
- ⅝ yd. purple batik for inner border
- 4 yds. for backing (pieced horizontally)
- ¾ yd. for binding
- 69" x 79" piece of batting

CUTTING

All measurements include ¼" seam allowances.

From assorted batiks, cut a total of:
- 50 squares, 6¼" x 6¼". Cut squares twice diagonally to yield 200 triangles (A) (you'll use 198).

From each of 8 assorted batiks, cut:
- 2 squares, 3⅜" x 3⅜" (16 total). Cut squares once diagonally to yield 32 triangles (C).

From the dark theme-print batik, cut:
- 9 strips, 5⅞" x 40"; crosscut strips into a total of 50 squares, 5⅞" x 5⅞". Cut squares once diagonally to yield 100 triangles (B) (you'll use 99).
- 2 strips, 3⅜" x 40"; crosscut strips into a total of 16 squares, 3⅜" x 3⅜". Cut squares once diagonally to yield 32 triangles (D).
- 1 strip, 5½" x 40"; crosscut strip into 16 rectangles, 1¾" x 5½" (E).
- 2 strips, 1¾" x 40"; crosscut strips into a total of 8 rectangles, 1¾" x 8" (F).
- 4 strips, 8" x 22" (G)
- 4 strips, 8" x 27" (H)

From the purple batik, cut:
- 8 strips, each 2" x 40"

From the fabric for binding, cut:
- 8 strips, 2½" x 40"

QUILT-TOP ASSEMBLY

1. On a design wall, arrange the large dark theme-print B triangles as shown opposite. Add the small assorted A triangles in groups of 4 matching triangles to form pinwheels. There will be partial pinwheels at the edges. Scatter the fabrics throughout the quilt top to form a balanced and pleasing arrangement.

2. Sew the pairs of small A triangles together. Do a few pairs at a time and immediately place them back on the design wall so you don't lose track of where they go in the arrangement. Sew each triangle pair to its large dark theme-print B triangle.

3. Sew the squares together in rows. Press the seams in opposite directions from row to row. Join the rows.

BORDER ASSEMBLY AND FINISHING

1. Sew the purple 2" strips together end to end. From the long strip, cut 2 pieces, 55½" long, for side border strips, and 2 pieces, 48½" long, for top and bottom border strips. Sew the side border strips to opposite sides of the quilt, and then add the top and bottom border strips. Press the seams toward the border.

2. Sew the assorted C and dark theme-print D triangles together in pairs. Sew 4 matching pairs together. Make 8 small pinwheels.

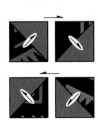

Make 8.

3. Sew a dark theme-print E rectangle to opposite sides of each small pinwheel. Sew a dark theme-print F rectangle to the top and bottom edges of 4 pinwheel units.

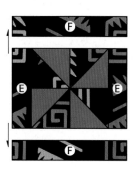

Side block for border
Make 4.

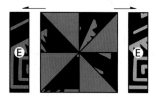

Corner block
Make 4.

4. Assemble the top and bottom border strips as shown below, using the 8" x 22" dark theme-print G strips. Assemble the 2 side border strips using the 8" x 27" dark theme-print H strips.

5. Pin and sew the side border strips to the quilt top. Pin and sew the remaining border strips to the top and bottom of the quilt top.

6. Referring to "Finishing" (page 27), layer the quilt top with batting and backing; baste. Quilt as desired. Bind the edges; add a label.

Make 2 top and bottom border strips.

Make 2 side borders strips.

SPRING RENDEZVOUS

SPRING RENDEZVOUS by Laurie Shifrin, 2000, Seattle, Washington, 55½" x 80½". Machine quilted by Gretchen Engle. Like a breath of fresh air, the colors in this quilt suggest a leisurely spring day. The numerous appliqués are simple to make, but if you choose to leave some out, the quilt will not lose its charm. The checkerboard borders add a sweet simplicity that will make this a favorite.

Skill Level: Intermediate

FINISHED QUILT SIZE

55½" x 80½"

MATERIALS

40"-wide fabric

- 1 yd. each of 8 assorted blue and green batiks for blocks, appliqués, and borders
- ½ yd. blue batik for center block
- 5 yds. for backing (pieced vertically)
- ¾ yd. for binding
- 61" x 86" piece of batting

CUTTING

All measurements include ¼" seam allowances.

To cut flower appliqués A through H, see "Appliqué Assembly," step 1 (right).

From the 8 assorted blue and green batiks, cut a total of:

- 4 squares, 10½ x 10½"
- 16 rectangles, 5½" x 10½"
- 70 squares, 5½" x 5½"
- 64 squares, 3" x 3" (in pairs of the same fabric)
- 480 squares, 1¾" x 1¾" (240 from blue and 240 from green)

From the blue batik, cut:

- 1 rectangle, 15½" x 20½"

From fabric for binding, cut:

- 8 strips, 2½" x 40"

APPLIQUÉ ASSEMBLY

1. Referring to "Appliqué" (page 22) and using flower template patterns A through H (page 97), cut and prepare the appliqué pieces listed below. Remember to add ¼" when cutting the fabric as patterns do not include seam allowances. An "r" means reverse template pattern.

   - 15 and 9 reversed of piece A (3 matching pieces for each flower)
   - 8 of piece B
   - 48 of piece C (8 matching pieces for each flower)
   - 6 of piece D
   - 2 and 3 reversed of piece E
   - 2 and 3 reversed of piece F
   - 6 and 6 reversed of G (1 matching G and Gr for each flower)
   - 6 of piece H (1 piece to match each set of G and Gr pieces)

2. Referring to the layout guides (opposite) for placement and appliqué order, make the following appliqué blocks:

   - Flower 1: Make 6 blocks (reverse 4) using 5½" squares for the background
   - Flower 2: Make 4 blocks using 10½" squares for the background
   - Flower 3: Make 5 blocks (reverse 3) using 5½" x 10½" rectangles for the background
   - Center flower block: Make 1 using the 15½" x 20½" rectangle for the background

3. Press the appliquéd blocks when complete.

Flower 1
Make 4.   Make 2.

Flower 2
Make 4.

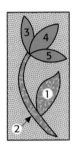

Flower 3
Make 2.   Make 3.

Center flower block
Make 1.

QUILT-TOP ASSEMBLY AND FINISHING

1. Sew a blue and a green 1¾" square together. Repeat to make 240 units for the inner and middle pieced borders.

Make 240.

2. Sew the units together, alternating the blue and green squares, to make the following:
   - 2 strips of 12 units each for inner top and bottom borders, starting with a green-and-blue unit
   - 2 strips of 20 units each for inner side borders, starting with a blue-and-green unit
   - 2 strips of 32 units each for outer top and bottom borders, starting with a blue-and-green unit
   - 2 strips of 56 units each for outer side borders, starting with a green-and-blue unit

   NOTE: *In a green-and-blue unit, the green square is on top of the blue square. In a blue-and-green unit, the blue square is on top of the green square.*

3. Sew the 12-unit checkerboard strips to the top and bottom edges of the center rectangle. Sew the 20-unit checkerboard strips to the sides of the rectangle.

4. To make a four-patch unit, sew together four 3" squares, 2 each from 2 different fabrics. Make 16 four-patch units.

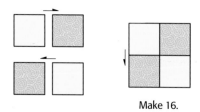

Make 16.

5. Arrange all the pieces into sections as shown. Shift similar-sized blocks around until you have a pleasing arrangement and no 2 pieces of the same fabric are touching. Sew the pieces within each group together, matching seams where applicable.

6. Sew the completed groups together in horizontal rows. Join the rows.

7. Sew the 32-unit checkerboard strips to the top and bottom of the quilt top. Sew the 56-unit checkerboard strips to the sides.

8. Sew the remaining 5½" squares together to make 2 border strips of 9 squares each and 2 border strips of 16 squares each.

9. Sew the shorter border strips to the top and bottom of the quilt top. Sew the longer border strips to the sides.

10. Referring to "Finishing" (page 27), layer the quilt top with batting and backing; baste. Quilt as desired. Bind the edges; add a label.

TIP: To make this quilt crib-sized, stop before you get to the second checkerboard round.

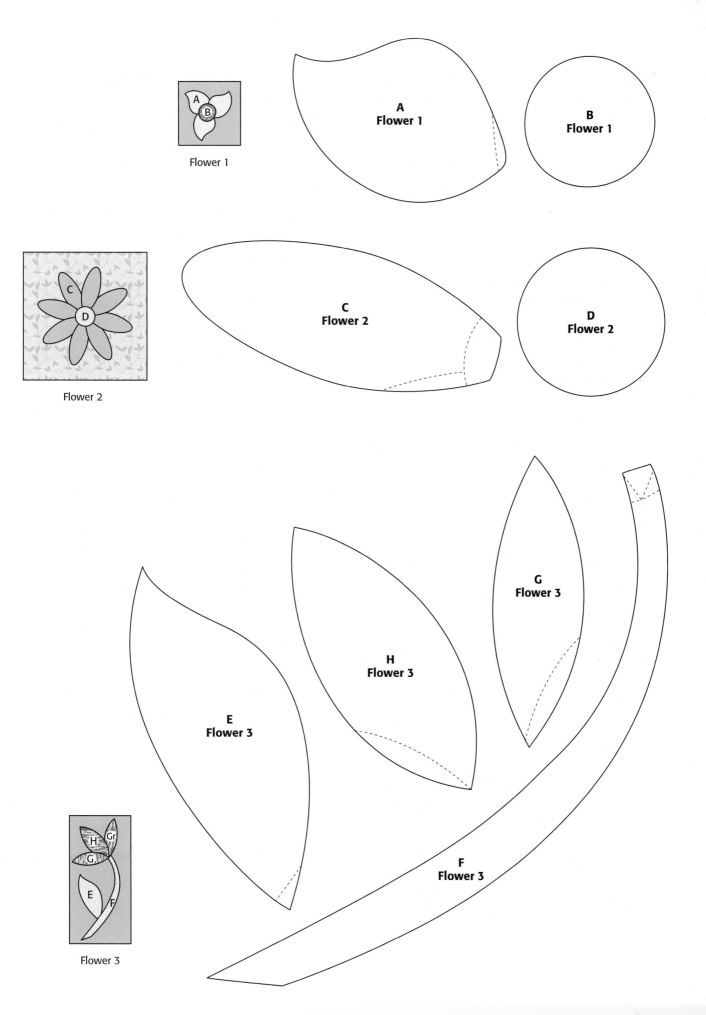

Flower 1

A
Flower 1

B
Flower 1

Flower 2

C
Flower 2

D
Flower 2

G
Flower 3

H
Flower 3

E
Flower 3

F
Flower 3

Flower 3

BYZANTINE STARS

BYZANTINE STARS by Laurie Shifrin, 2000, Seattle, Washington, 59½" x 75½". Machine quilted by Sherry Rogers. The lines and order of Byzantine architecture characterize the primary star pattern. The dramatic contrast of darks and lights reveals a secondary interplay of stars and movement, while the subtle background colors spill over into the border.

FINISHED QUILT SIZE

59½" x 75½"

MATERIALS

40"-wide fabric

- 2½ yds. blue-print batik for piecing and outer border
- 1½ yds. brown batik for piecing
- 1 yd. dark blue batik for piecing and middle border)
- 1 yd. cream-dot batik for piecing and inner border
- 1⅜ yds. slate batik for piecing
- 4¾ yds. for backing (pieced vertically)
- ¾ yd. for binding
- 65" x 81" piece of batting

CUTTING

All measurements include ¼" seam allowances.

Make pieces G, H, I, and J (page 102) referring to "Machine-Piecing Templates" (page 22).

From the blue-print batik, cut:

Along the lengthwise grain:
- 4 strips, 5" wide by fabric length

Along the crosswise grain of remaining fabric (approximately 20" wide):
- 3 strips, 4¾" x 20"; crosscut strips into a total of 12 squares, 4¾" x 4¾" (A).
- 4 strips, 2¾" x 20"; from strips, cut 14 and 14 reversed of piece H.
- 5 strips, 3½" x 20"; crosscut strips into a total of 24 squares, 3½" x 3½" (F).
- 7 strips, 3½" x 20"; crosscut strips into a total of 48 rectangles, 2½" x 3½" (E).

From the brown batik, cut:

- 3 strips, 3⅞" x 40"; crosscut strips into a total of 24 squares, 3⅞" x 3⅞". Cut squares once diagonally to yield 48 triangles (B).

- 5 strips, 6" x 40"; from strips, cut 48 and 48 reversed of piece J.

From the dark blue batik, cut:

- 2 strips, 3¾" x 40"; from strips, cut 48 of piece I.
- 2 strips, 2⅞" x 40"; crosscut strips into a total of 24 squares, 2⅞" x 2⅞" (D).
- 8 strips, ⅞" x 40"

From the cream-dot batik, cut:

- 2 strips, 2¾" x 40"; from strips, cut 48 of piece G.
- 2 strips, 2⅞" x 40"; crosscut strips into a total of 24 squares, 2⅞" x 2⅞" (C).
- 8 strips, 1⅛" x 40"

From the slate batik, cut:

- 4 strips, 2¾" x 40"; from strips, cut 34 and 34 reversed of piece H.
- 3 strips, 3½" x 40"; crosscut strips into a total of 24 squares, 3½" x 3½" (F).
- 5 strips, 2½" x 40"; crosscut strips into a total of 48 rectangles, 2½" x 3½" (E).

From the fabric for binding, cut:

- 8 strips, 2½" x 40"

QUILT-TOP ASSEMBLY

1. With a sharp pencil, mark the ¼" intersection points on the wrong side of pieces G, H, I, and J.

2. Sew 2 brown B triangles to opposite sides of a blue-print A square. Sew 2 brown B triangles to the remaining sides of the A square. Make 12 units.

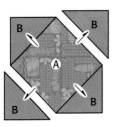

Make 12.

3. Draw a diagonal line on the wrong side of each cream-dot C square. Pair each cream-dot square with a dark blue D square. Referring to "Half-Square-Triangle Units" (page 20), make 48 units.

Make 48.

4. Sew together 2 blue-print E rectangles, 1 blue-print F square, and 1 unit from step 3. Make 24 units. Repeat with slate E rectangles, slate F squares, and half-square-triangle units to make another 24 units.

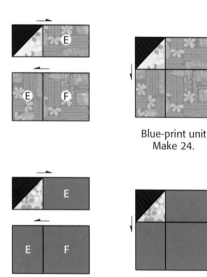

Blue-print unit
Make 24.

Slate unit
Make 24.

5. Sew the blue-print H and Hr triangles to the short sides of a cream-dot G triangle. Make 14 units. Repeat with slate H and Hr triangles and the remaining cream-dot G triangles to make 34 units.

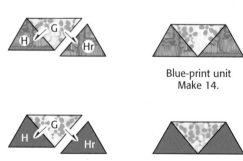

Blue-print unit
Make 14.

Slate unit
Make 34.

6. Sew a dark blue I triangle to each unit made in step 5. Add a brown J and a brown Jr triangle to the sides. Make 14 blue-print units and 34 slate units.

 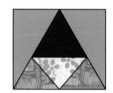

Blue-print unit
Make 14.

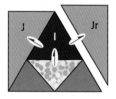 

Slate unit
Make 34.

7. Arrange the units by color as shown to make 2 center blocks, 6 side blocks, and 4 corner blocks.

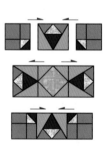 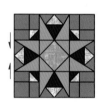

Center block
Make 2.

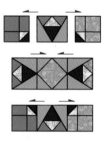 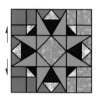

Side block
Make 6.

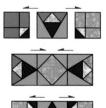

Corner block
Make 4.

8. Arrange the 12 blocks as shown. Sew the blocks together in rows. Join the rows.

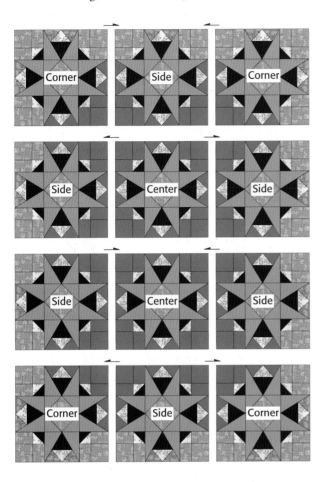

BORDER ASSEMBLY AND FINISHING

1. Sew the 1⅛" x 40" inner-border strips together end to end in pairs. Sew the ⅞" x 40" middle-border strips together in pairs. Sew an inner-, middle-, and 5"-wide outer-border strip together. Make 4 border strips.

2. Referring to "Mitered Borders" (page 25), sew the 4 border strips to the quilt top and miter the corners.

3. Referring to "Finishing" (page 27), layer the quilt top with batting and backing; baste. Quilt as desired. Bind the edges; add a label.

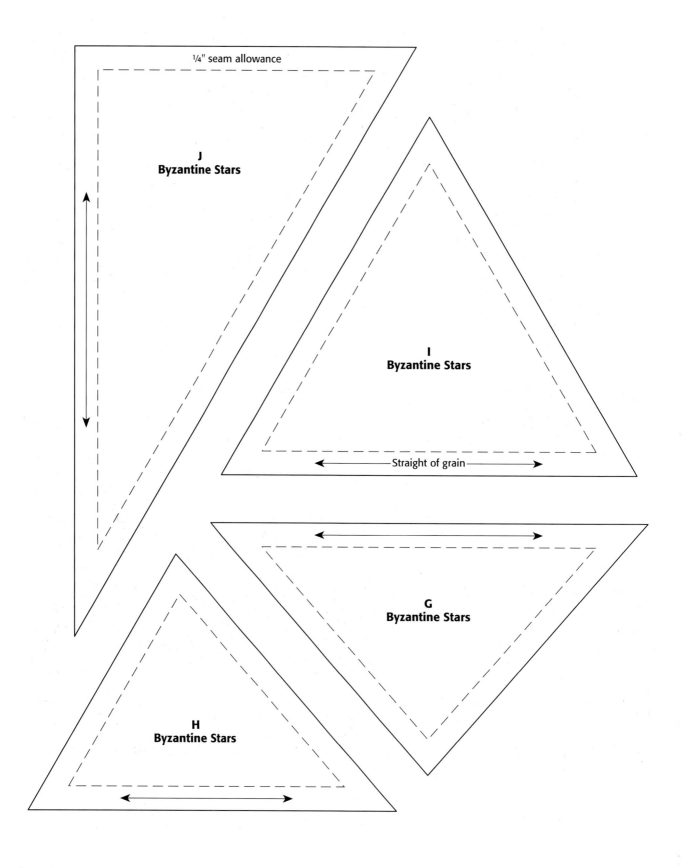

¼" seam allowance

J
Byzantine Stars

I
Byzantine Stars

Straight of grain

G
Byzantine Stars

H
Byzantine Stars

PERSIAN FANTASY

Pᴇʀsɪᴀɴ FANTASY by Laurie Shifrin, 2000, Seattle, Washington, 75½" x 75½". Machine quilted by Gretchen Engle. This stunning quilt mixes batik and nonbatik fabrics in the simple but intoxicating Milky Way block. The illusion of motion is created by setting the blocks to form concentric diamonds. The lush colors—plum, gold, red, and peach—are tied together by the gorgeous border fabric.

FINISHED QUILT SIZE

75½" x 75½"

MATERIALS

40"-wide fabric

- From center out, for piecing:
  - Fabric 1: ⅞ yd. plum batik for squares and inner border
  - Fabric 2: ½ yd. peach-and-yellow vine batik
  - Fabric 3: ⅝ yd. burgundy swirl print
  - Fabric 4: ⅞ yd. yellow mumm batik
  - Fabric 5: 1⅛ yd. red fire batik
  - Fabric 6: 1⅛ yd. black-and-red speckled print
  - Fabric 7: 1⅛ yd. yellow paisley print
  - Fabric 8: ¾ yd. magenta batik
  - Fabric 9: ⅝ yd. mottled batik
  - Fabric 10: ⅓ yd. gold chevron batik
- 2½ yds. large gold print for outer border
- 4¾ yds. for backing
- ⅞ yd. for binding
- 81" x 81" piece of batting

CUTTING

All measurements include ¼" seam allowances.

Make the Triangle Template (page 108) referring to "Machine-Piecing Templates" (page 22).

For easy reference, cut a small piece from the selvage of each of fabrics 1–10 and tape the pieces in order to a piece of paper; number them 1–10.

Cut strips and squares as follows, across fabric width:

	3½" strips	Crosscut into 3½" squares	3⅞" strips	Crosscut into 3⅞" squares	2" strips
Fabric 1	—	—	1	2	1
Fabric 2	1	4	1	8	2
Fabric 3	1	8	2	16	2
Fabric 4	2	12	3	24	3
Fabric 5	2	16	4	32	4
Fabric 6	2	20	4	40	5
Fabric 7	2	12	4	28	4
Fabric 8	1	8	3	20	3
Fabric 9	1	4	2	12	2
Fabric 10	—	—	1	4	1

From fabric 1, also cut:

- 1 square, 3½" x 3½", from the remainder of the 3⅞" strip
- 8 strips, 2" x 40"
- 1 strip, 2⅜" x 40"; crosscut strip into 4 rectangles, 2⅜" x 7".

From the large gold print, cut:

- 1 strip, 3⅞" x 40"; crosscut strip into 2 squares, each 3⅞" x 3⅞". Cut squares once diagonally to yield 4 half-square triangles. From the remainder of the strip, cut 8 rectangles, 2" x 3½", and 8 squares, 2" x 2".
- 1 strip, 2⅜" x 40"; crosscut strip into 4 rectangles, 2⅜" x 7".
- 1 strip, 3½" x 40"; crosscut strip into 4 rectangles, 3½" x 9½".
- 8 strips, 8" x 40"

From the fabric for binding, cut:

- 9 strips, 2½" x 40"

QUILT-TOP ASSEMBLY

1. Sew the 2" x 40" strips of fabrics 1 through 10 together into strip sets as indicated; then cut the strip sets into 2"-wide segments. Press each seam toward the odd-numbered fabric.

	Strip sets	2" segments
Fabrics 1 and 2	1	4
Fabrics 2 and 3	1	12
Fabrics 3 and 4	1	12
Fabrics 4 and 5	2	28
Fabrics 5 and 6	2	36
Fabrics 6 and 7	2	36
Fabrics 7 and 8	2	28
Fabrics 8 and 9	1	20
Fabrics 9 and 10	1	16

2. Sew the segments made in step 1 together, being sure to orient each pair as indicated in the illustration and chart. Make a total of 100 four-patch units.

Strip-set segments	Four-patch units
Fabrics 3 and 2 Fabrics 2 and 1	4
Fabrics 4 and 3 Fabrics 3 and 2	8
Fabrics 5 and 4 Fabrics 4 and 3	12
Fabrics 6 and 5 Fabrics 5 and 4	16
Fabrics 7 and 6 Fabrics 6 and 5	20
Fabrics 8 and 7 Fabrics 7 and 6	16
Fabrics 9 and 8 Fabrics 8 and 7	12
Fabrics 10 and 9 Fabrics 9 and 8	8
Fabrics 9 and 10 Fabrics 10 and 9	4

3. Referring to "Half-Square-Triangle Units" (page 20) and using $3\frac{7}{8}$" squares, make 180 half-square-triangle units as indicated.

	$3\frac{7}{8}$" squares	Half-square- triangle units
Fabrics 1 and 2	2 each	4
Fabrics 2 and 3	6 each	12
Fabrics 3 and 4	10 each	20
Fabrics 4 and 5	14 each	28
Fabrics 5 and 6	18 each	36
Fabrics 6 and 7	16 each	32
Fabrics 7 and 8	12 each	24
Fabrics 8 and 9	8 each	16
Fabrics 9 and 10	4 each	8

4. Arrange the plain squares, half-square-triangle units, and four-patch units as shown. Take special care with fabric orientation. Once everything is in the right place, sew the units together into rows. Press the seams away from the half-square-triangle units. Join the rows.

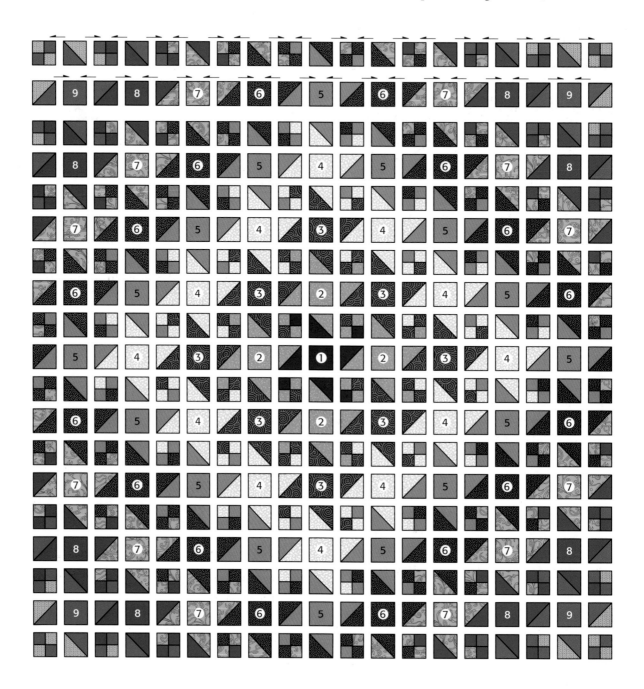

BORDER ASSEMBLY AND FINISHING

1. Sew a 2⅜" x 7" fabric 1 rectangle to each 2⅜" x 7" gold-print rectangle. Make 4 units. Cut both ends of the unit to straighten the edges. Use the Triangle Template (page 108) to cut 2 triangles from each unit as shown. Be sure to align the tip of the triangle with the edge of the unit, and the line on the template with the seam on the unit. Keep the template right side up to cut both triangles.

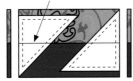

Match line on template with seam line.

Make 4 units.
Cut 8 triangles.

2. Cut the 6 remaining 3⅞" fabric 6 squares once diagonally to yield 12 triangles. Sew a fabric 6 triangle to each triangle made in step 1. Sew each remaining fabric 6 triangle to a gold-print triangle.

Make 4.   Make 4.   Make 4.

3. From the remaining 2"-wide fabric 6 strips, cut 8 squares, 2" x 2". Sew each 2" fabric 6 square to a 2" gold-print square. Sew a 3½" x 2" gold-print rectangle to each of these units.

Make 8.

4. Sew together 3 units from step 2, 2 units from step 3, one 3½" x 9½" gold-print rectangle, and one 3½" fabric 6 square. Make 4 center border squares.

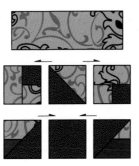 

Make 4.

5. Sew each 2" x 40" inner-border strip to an outer-border strip. Trim the left edge on 4 of the strips. Trim the right edge on the 4 remaining strips.

Cut 4 this way.

Cut 4 this way.

6. Sew a border strip to each side of a center border square, aligning the clean-cut edges with the square.

7. Referring to "Mitered Borders" (page 25), pin and sew the borders to the quilt top, matching the seams of the center border square with the seams of the block in the quilt top.

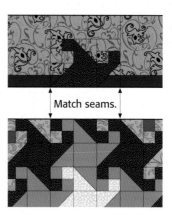

Match seams.

8. Referring to "Finishing" (page 27), layer the quilt top with batting and backing; baste. Quilt as desired. Bind the edges; add a label.

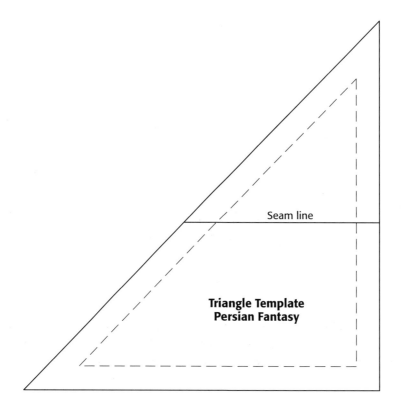

Seam line

**Triangle Template
Persian Fantasy**

STEPPING OUT

STEPPING OUT by Laurie Shifrin, 2000, Seattle, Washington, 57" x 57". Nine Patch blocks in a variety of rich colors form a chain against a lively pink background. The pieced outer border gives the fabric collector an opportunity to use small bits of lots of different fabrics. Note how the pink background squares seem to "walk away" to the corners of the quilt.

FINISHED QUILT SIZE

57" x 57"

MATERIALS

40"-wide fabric

- ½ yd. each of 8 or more assorted purple- and green-print batiks for blocks and borders
- 1⅜ yds. pink batik for background
- ⅞ yd. burgundy-print batik for center of Nine Patch blocks and inner borders
- 3¾ yd. for backing
- ⅝ yd. for binding
- 63" x 63" piece of batting

CUTTING

All measurements include ¼" seam allowances.

From the assorted purple- and green-print batiks, cut a total of:

- 24 sets of 4 matching squares, 2" x 2" (B, 96 total)
- 8 rectangles, 2¼" x 5" (K)
- 8 rectangles, 2" x 3½" (L)
- 8 rectangles, 1¾" x 2¼" (M)
- 8 rectangles, 1½" x 1¼" (N)
- 56 rectangles, 1¾" x 3" (inner border)
- 88 rectangles, 2½" x 6¾" (outer border)

From the pink batik, cut:

- 3 strips, 2½" x 40"; crosscut strips into a total of 96 rectangles, 2½" x 2" (C).
- 4 strips, 5½" x 40"; crosscut strips into a total of 25 squares, 5½" x 5½" (D).
- 1 strip, 5" x 40"; crosscut strip into 4 squares, 5" x 5" (E), 4 squares, 2¼" x 2¼" (F), and 4 squares, 2" x 2" (G).
- 1 strip, 1¾" x 40"; crosscut strip into 4 squares, 1¾" x 1¾" (H), 4 squares, 1½" x 1½" (I), and 4 squares, 1¼" x 1¼" (J).

From the burgundy-print batik, cut:

- 2 strips, 2½" x 40"; crosscut strips into a total of 24 squares, 2½" x 2½" (A).
- 4 strips, 2" x 35½"
- 4 strips, 2¼" x 35½"

From fabric for binding, cut:

- 7 strips, 2½" x 40"

QUILT-TOP ASSEMBLY

1. Arrange and sew together 4 matching purple or green B squares, 4 pink C rectangles, and 1 burgundy-print A square to make an uneven Nine Patch block. Make 24 blocks.

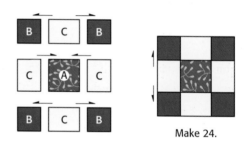

Make 24.

2. Arrange the Nine Patch blocks and pink D squares as shown. Distribute fabrics randomly throughout the quilt top. Sew the blocks together in rows. Join the rows.

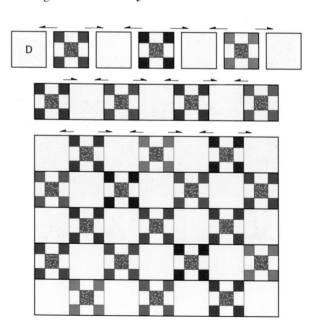

BORDER ASSEMBLY AND FINISHING

1. For the inner border, sew 14 assorted purple and green 1¾" x 3" rectangles together, end to end; mix up the fabrics for a random yet balanced look. Sew a 2" burgundy-print strip and a 2¼" burgundy-print strip to opposite sides of each pieced border strip. Make 4 inner-border strips.

2"
2¼"

Make 4.

2. Sew 2 pieced inner-border strips to opposite sides of the quilt top, placing the 2"-wide strip next to the center of the quilt. Sew a pink E square to each end of the remaining strips and sew these to the top and bottom edges, again placing the 2"-wide strip next to the center of the quilt.

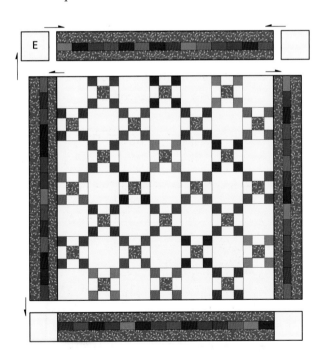

3. Arrange and sew pieces F through N as shown. Make 4 corner blocks.

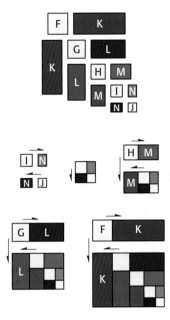

4. For the outer border, sew together 22 assorted 2½" x 6¾" rectangles. Make 4 pieced outer-border strips. Sew 2 outer-border strips to opposite sides of the quilt top. Sew a corner block to each end of the remaining strips and sew these to the top and bottom edges of the quilt top.

5. Referring to "Finishing" (page 27), layer the quilt top with batting and backing; baste. Quilt as desired. Bind the edges and add a label.

ABOUT THE AUTHOR

EVER SINCE she learned from her mother how to sew clothing in her early teens, Laurie Shifrin has loved creating things out of fabric.

While studying violin at a music conservatory in Connecticut, and later as she began her professional violin career, Laurie worked in various fabric and quilting stores. During this period she completed her first quilt, called "Giant Dahlia."

From then on, she focused her sewing efforts on quilting and learned new techniques and designs. Soon she was custom-quilting and designing her own quilts. In the late 1980s, when severe tendinitis in both arms forced her to end her violin career (and temporarily stopped any sewing activity), Laurie went back to college and attained an MBA, focusing on marketing and arts administration.

After working in the administration of a major symphony orchestra for four years, Laurie embarked on another lifestyle change. She took a job at In The Beginning, a wonderful quilt store in Seattle, Washington, where she now lives. Starting as a salesclerk, she went on to become teacher, sample maker, and pattern tester. Then, while preparing the text for this book, Laurie was appointed retail manager.

In addition to the quilts Laurie has created for In The Beginning, she hand quilted the cover quilt of *Threads from the '30s*, compiled by Nancy J. Martin. One of her original quilts was published in Sandy Bonsib's book *Quilting Your Memories*. *Batik Beauties* is Laurie's first quilting book.